Inviting Positive Classroom Discipline

D1365976

National Middle School Association *is dedicated to improving the educational experiences of young adolescents by providing vision, knowledge, and resources to all who serve them in order to develop healthy, productive, and ethical citizens.*

INVITING POSITIVE CLASSROOM DISCIPLINE

by

William Watson Purkey
and
David B. Strahan

National Middle School Association
Westerville, Ohio

LB
3013
P86
2002

National Middle School Association
4151 Executive Parkway
Suite 300
Westerville, Ohio 43081
Telephone (800) 528-NMSA

Copyright ©2002 by National Middle School Association.

All rights reserved. No part of this publication may be reproduced or transmitted in any form or by any means, electronic or mechanical, without permission in writing from the publisher except in the case of brief quotations embodied in reviews or articles. The materials presented herein are the expressions of the authors and do not necessarily represent the policies of NMSA. NMSA is a registered servicemark of National Middle School Association.

Printed in the United States of America.

Sue Swaim, Executive Director
Jeff Ward, Deputy Executive Director
Edward Brazee, Editor, Professional Publications
John Lounsbury, Consulting Editor, Professional Publications
Mary Mitchell, Designer, Editorial Assistant
Marcia Meade-Hurst, Senior Publications Representative
Mark Shumaker, Cover Design

Library of Congress Cataloging-in-Publication Data
Purkey, William Watson.

Inviting positive classroom discipline/by William Watson Purkey and David B. Strahan.
p. cm.
Includes bibliographical references.
ISBN 1-56090-129-2 (pbk.)
1. Classroom management. 2. School discipline. I. Strahan, David B. II. Title.

LB3013 .P86 2002
371.102'4--dc21 2002141552.

CONTENTS

FOREWORD

nce again, when the 33rd Annual PDK/Gallup Poll asked respondents to identify the biggest problem facing local public schools, "lack of discipline/more control" was right up there at the top, tied for first place this year with "lack of financial support/funding/money."

The perennial nature of discipline as the most serious school problem is both discouraging and surprising. Discouraging because lack of discipline is a major impediment to effective teaching and learning; and surprising because the topic has been receiving vast amounts of attention in both preservice and inservice programs. In addition, a raft of books, each touting a particular discipline plan or strategy, has been published in recent years.

However, *Inviting Positive Classroom Discipline* is not just another in the series of advocacies few of which have captured the hearts and minds of teachers sufficiently to solve this persistent problem. Because it is based on a sound theory, one that will prevent problems rather than just treat symptoms, this book holds real promise for initiating actions that will begin to turn the tide.

Applying the valid and positive theory of Invitational Education to managing student behavior, Purkey and Strahan spin a most engaging treatise. Using the easy-to-identify-with metaphor of orange and blue cards, they present a color-coded approach to classroom management, one that is pure "middle school." With dozens of specific, practical ideas in the form of "blue notes" scattered throughout, this volume is easy to read, even fun to read; but, make no mistake about it, what is presented is a very serious and thoughtful approach to improving the behavior of students in classroom situations. It does this by creating a climate that brings to the forefront the best of human nature.

This small volume also comes with a bonus; for although focused on discipline, readers who instill in their attitudes and actions the advocacies of Invitational Education will discover that they have, at the same time, created a classroom environment that will greatly improve instruction and student achievement! It would be a mistake to pass this book by, thinking it is just another rhetoric-rich but practice-poor program for controlling students' behavior. Seldom does a resource offer so much in so few pages. Accept the invitation that is offered here.

— John H. Lounsbury

1.

INVITATIONAL TEACHING: A COLOR-CODED APPROACH TO CLASSROOM MANAGEMENT

Successful teachers "invite" positive discipline based on their understanding of themselves and their students as well as on practical, concrete, and specific strategies for accomplishing this goal. This book differs from other books on classroom discipline in that it offers both a theory of practice for inviting positive classroom discipline and a color-coded metaphor to guide that practice. The theory is "Invitational Teaching," and the metaphor is "blue and orange cards." *Inviting Positive Classroom Discipline* describes both the "why" (Invitational Teaching) and the "how" (the blue and orange metaphor) of successful classroom management. Both concepts will be explained in this chapter.

We have found that the metaphor of blue and orange cards provides a powerful framework for describing the underlying processes that shape a truly inviting school environment. To illustrate these underlying processes, we share a number of examples we have drawn from our own experiences and our work with hundreds of teachers over the past three decades. These illustrations document the "artistry" of great teaching.

Gathered in a wide range of settings over an extended period of time, these illustrations demonstrate ways that teachers put theory into practice. While these teachers may not have known or used the language of Invitational Teaching, they share a set of core beliefs that shape the decisions they make in their classrooms. *Inviting Positive Classroom Discipline* captures some of the dynamics of their success and links those dynamics with our research on inviting positive discipline.

To share these insights in concrete ways throughout the book, we present a series of "blue notes" such as the one below. These offer specific suggestions for inviting positive classroom discipline.

> *BE POSITIVE AND PRESCRIPTIVE. Studies of successful teachers show that they consistently monitor performance and expect good results. They do so in ways that are positive and prescriptive rather than punitive. Reminding students of agreements and expectations in a firm and gentle fashion allows them to feel more responsible and keeps lines of communication open.* ♪

As helpful as blue notes are, they are insufficient by themselves. Knowing *what* to do to maintain classroom discipline is not enough. *Practical expediency is no match for explicit theory.* To be of maximum value, blue notes must be anchored in an understanding of *why* they lead to successful classroom management.

The why of positive classroom management is explained by an emerging theory of practice called Invitational Teaching. This model was first presented by Purkey (1978) and enriched by the research and writing of many scholars, including Amos (1985), Novak (1992, 1994, 2002), Schmidt (1994), Stanley (1992), and others. Invitational Teaching has been successfully applied in addressing such concerns as academic achievement (Purkey & Novak, 1996; Stanley & Purkey,

1994), safe schools (Purkey, 2000), and leadership (Purkey & Siegel, 2002).

Invitational Teaching

Simply stated, Invitational Teaching is a theory of practice. It maintains that every person and everything in and around schools adds to, or subtracts from, the process of being a beneficial presence in the lives of human beings. It addresses the total educational environment and culture of the classroom and school. Ideally, the five powerful "P's" of *people, places, policies, programs,* and *processes* that constitute any school culture should be so intentionally inviting as to create an educational world that encourages each individual to succeed. Everyone who enters this world is summoned cordially to develop intellectually, socially, physically, psychologically, and spiritually. Invitational Teaching is a process for communicating caring and appropriate messages intended to nurture the realization of human potential as well as for identifying and changing those forces that defeat and destroy potential.

A basic and somewhat radical assumption of Invitational Teaching relates to human motivation. This radical assumption is that there is only one kind of human motivation – an internal and continuous incentive that every person has at all time, in all places, during all activities. People are always motivated; in fact, they are never unmotivated. Students may not do what we would prefer them to do, but it can never be said that they are unmotivated. This view of motivation is a tremendous advantage for those who practice Invitational Teaching. Rather than spending endless amounts of time and energy trying to "motivate" students, Invitational Teachers seek to guide students' intrinsic energy. The goal is to invite them to see themselves as capable of tackling tough challenges, overcoming obstacles, accomplishing great things, and behave accordingly.

Countless books on discipline have encouraged teachers to "motivate," "reinforce," "empower," "turn on," "build," "enhance," and "shape" students. This kind of "doing to" language is metaphorically appropriate for working with objects and machines, but not people. As well intentioned as the authors of these books may be, their writings suggest that they view students as objects to be moved here and there as checkers on a checkerboard, as functionaries in a system. There are obvious dangers in the "objectification" of people. Such thinking denies or reduces their humanity. A "doing-to" mentality is the opposite of Invitational Teaching.

Objects are used, people are invited. From an Invitational Teaching perspective, students are able, valuable, and responsible and should be treated accordingly. This viewpoint is reflected in such respectful language as "offer," "propose," "present," "summon," "invite," and "consider." The words teachers use to describe behavior influence the way they and their students think and behave in the classroom.

USE INCLUSIVE PRONOUNS. Using such pronouns as "we," "us," and "our" is much more likely to encourage a sense of classroom community than "you," "mine," and "yours." For example, saying "We've got to get down to business if we're going to finish this work" is preferable to "You students must complete your work." Using the collective term promotes shared effort and responsibility. ♪

Becoming an Invitational Teacher

While many of today's teachers find their careers satisfying, other teachers find themselves in less fortunate situations, swamped with responsibilities that appear to have little relevance to education. These include keeping all sorts of daily records as well as locker checks, hall monitoring, lunchroom patrol – and a host of other assignments that do not involve teaching. Teachers could more easily accept such duties if these non-teaching responsibilities were not coupled with crowded classes, schedules without breaks, low salaries, high stakes testing, dilapidated facilities, zero-tolerance policies, less-than-enthusiastic colleagues, remote administrators, and students who seem to reject the most well-intentioned invitations. Faced with such rejections, teachers can easily become disillusioned, bitter, and dejected. They begin to think: "Why should I continue to invite students and colleagues when my invitations are rarely accepted?" When this thinking takes over, another teacher with great potential joins the ranks of those living a professional half-life, burdened by the loss of idealism and spirit. Such loss need not happen. Teachers who approach students and colleagues with a consistent theory of practice learn to conserve and focus their energies and reduce the likelihood they will feel intimidated or overwhelmed.

Becoming an Invitational Teacher requires a definite point of view. Many in education tend to think of teaching as something that the teacher does to students. The teacher, by virtue of having authority and power, issues orders and directs students. No matter how kind, caring, and generous the teacher may be, the process is still the command-and-control variety. By contrast, Invitational Teachers turn toward others with a generous and genuine attitude of respect, trust, optimism, and intentionality. They seek collaboration with students on important projects of mutual benefit.

FOLLOW SEVEN SIMPLE TIPS.

1. *Dress better than your students do.*
2. *Begin and end class on time.*
3. *Provide success experiences.*
4. *Plan lessons ahead.*
5. *Keep your cool.*
6. *Be consistent.*
7. *Be professional.*♪

Invitational Teaching begins with a particular "stance," defined as the theoretical position from which the teacher operates. This stance largely determines his or her level of personal and professional functioning. In sports such as baseball or tennis, a stance represents readiness for action. A teacher's stance in the classroom, while less visible, is equally important. When applied to Invitational Teaching, the stance offers the teacher an attitudinal structure and direction that creates and maintains a productive classroom environment.

A consistent stance is critical in times of stress. As Reed and Strahan (1995) note, "In hostile situations, it is often best to be gentle. Hostage negotiators speak softly. Bank tellers remain calm during a robbery. SWAT teams try to talk through confrontations" (p. 321). This same "strong yet gentle" stance is equally powerful in the classroom.

A teacher we know reported an incident that demonstrates the importance of thinking invitationally, even in a potentially dangerous situation. As students gathered in the hallway before a Saturday enrichment class, he noticed a circle of boys laughing uneasily. When he walked closer, he saw a flash of steel as one of the students turned away from the others. He asked the others to go in the classroom and very calmly asked the student to explain what he had under his jacket. The student replied that he had brought his grandfather's fishing knife to show his friends. The teacher asked him to give him the knife and then explained that he would have to report the incident to the school's safety officer. The student begged him not to report it and repeated over and over "I wasn't going to do anything with it." As they waited for the officer to arrive, the teacher calmly explained "That might be the case, but we have rules regarding anything that could be a weapon." The teacher told us later that "The tough part came when the parents arrived. His dad was furious with him and his mom kept crying. I told them that we know he was not likely to hurt anyone and that we had faith in his ability to work through this. During his suspension, I called the family every other day or so. When he came back to school, I tried to spend a little extra time with him. He has been well behaved since."

FORM TRIADS. Divide the class into groups of threes called "triads." Ask each triad to research, obtain materials, and teach a mini-lesson on selected course content. Placing a student who is having behavior difficulties with two well-behaved peers invites new friendships, breaks down barriers, and provides role models for the rambunctious youngster. ♪

Instances like this show that teachers can continue to send messages that "you are valuable, able, and responsible," even when students make bad choices. This teacher's actions showed that "I care about you as a person even though I cannot accept this particular action." Over time, these messages communicate respect and promote self-discipline.

Invitational Teachers seek to enroll students in a vision of greatness – to offer them a vivid and compelling picture of their relatively boundless potential in all areas of worthwhile human endeavor. This vision is founded on certain principles that serve as a conceptual framework to assist teachers in their efforts to communicate their vision and to summon students to realize their potential as learners.

There are four theoretical principles (values) that give Invitational Teaching direction and purpose. Together, these four principles form a basic set of guiding beliefs and a particular stance that are echoed throughout this book. These are respect, trust, optimism, and intentionality. In the section that follows, we examine each of these four principles in detail and offer examples of ways teachers we know have demonstrated these principles in their practices. These examples show how beliefs can be enacted in powerful ways and, while it may be almost impossible to put each of these principles in action with every student all of the time, they represent the core values of Invitational Teaching.

Respect

The first principle of Invitational Teaching is that students are able, valuable, and responsible and should be treated accordingly. When students do not behave accordingly, it is assumed that they are capable of behaving so. Central to Invitational Teaching is an appreciation for the self-directing powers of each student. In Invitational Teaching, respect is given to each student whether or not the respect is "earned." Waiting for a student to earn respect before giving it would make about as much sense as a medical doctor waiting for patients to get well before he or she provides treatment. In Invitational Teaching, respect is a given – an undeniable birthright of each human being.

A corollary to the principle of respect is responsibility. In Invitational Teaching, each student is recognized as the world's greatest authority on himself or herself and is viewed as ultimately responsible for his or her own actions. Excuses do not free people from responsibilities. The student is ultimately responsible for his or her behavior.

HOLD STUDENTS ACCOUNTABLE. Definite expectations, in themselves, are a powerful invitation. Expectations inform students that they can and should take responsibility for their actions. "You make a mess, you clean it up." Accepting excuses sends the wrong message in the classroom and in life. ♪

Teachers who adopt Invitational Teaching use their energies to educate students on how to behave responsibly and then aid them in exercising their autonomy in socially acceptable ways. Students are given numerous opportunities to behave responsibly. Blind obedience and conformity without thinking are in opposition to respect for oneself and others. As Duke and Jones (1985) explained "Schools that help students develop their capacity to behave responsibly but deny them significant opportunities to utilize these skills are no more likely to foster responsibility than schools that provide ample opportunities for responsible behavior but little instruction in how to behave responsibly" (p. 278). Establishing a climate of accountability is a major way to encourage appropriate student behavior.

One additional component of respect is the belief that students have the ability to learn in school. Each student has relatively untapped energies for thinking, learning, choosing, and deciding. These capabilities can be realized in an optimally inviting classroom environment where there is respect for students and their self-directing abilities. Thus, Invitational Teachers seek to encourage good behavior *and* academic achievement.

Trust

Teachers establish trust through an inviting *pattern* of action, as opposed to a single inviting act. Rome was not built in a day and neither is trust. A teacher's consistent behavior creates trust which establishes a dependable classroom environment.

One of the most powerful ways that teachers communicate trust is how willing they are to share things that matter to them with their students. We know a teacher who collects valuable tea sets. Her husband travels overseas frequently, and when he does, he often brings home unique tea sets for her. Her collection includes porcelain from places like India, England, and China. Each spring, for a special event, her seventh graders plan and present a tea ceremony as part of their study of other cultures. She packs up her tea sets and brings them to school. Students use them to prepare and serve tea to their parents. It is one of the highlights of the year. When asked by a colleague if she was afraid that students would break them, she replied "I am more worried about packing them and bringing them in the car than I am about the students. They know how important they are to me, and they treat them with great care." Incidents like this show that she is treating her students with great care as well. By creating a climate of trust over time, she has reached a point where she can trust her students with possessions that are precious to her.

Johnston (1985) reported that "The very best schools are trusting places" (p. 7). According to Johnston, students feel this trust by having many opportunities to make decisions and by having guidelines to monitor their own behavior. In a trusting school environment, "emblems of trust" are everywhere. Doors are unlocked. Students handle valuable equipment. For example, students in one school are supplied with relatively expensive cameras to take photographs at home. Any lapse of responsible behavior is treated as a "learning exercise" (Johnston, p. 8). Students are asked to analyze their own actions and to make suggestions for future behavior.

SHARE DUTIES. There are numerous tasks that students can do to help manage the classroom. For example, distributing and collecting materials, preparing experiments, operating equipment, preparing reports are among many good ways to turn student energy into productive avenues and make life a little easier for the teacher. These activities encourage a feeling of trust. ♪

While trust is based on a dependable pattern of action by the teacher, even the smallest inviting act, which at the moment may appear to be of little or no consequence, can have far-reaching impact. Even the smallest act has boundless potential. A basic premise of Invitational Teaching is that everything counts. Human potential, though not always apparent, is always there...waiting to be discovered and invited forth.

Optimism

Invitational Teaching is based on a positive vision of human beings: that each person is able, valuable, capable of self-direction, and should be treated accordingly. This optimism is centered on the belief that the deepest urges of human existence are to be affirmed in one's present worth while being invited to realize one's potential. Optimism is more than a Pollyanna outlook on life. Rather, optimism is essential for development to occur. As Goethe explained, "If we take people as they are, we make them worse. If we treat them as if they were what they ought to be, we help them to become what they are capable of becoming" (reported in Frankl, 1968, p. 8).

When teachers make prophecies about their students, they are not predicting, they are creating. Because this is so, it is vital that teachers be romantics: to see things not just as they are but as they could be, to look at non-readers and see readers, look at non-athletes and see athletes, to look at misbehaving students and see their potential to be good citizens. Implicit assumptions of Invitational Teaching are that students want to learn, and that they *will* learn in a cooperative and supportive environment. Invitational Teachers believe that they are capable of creating and maintaining such a classroom atmosphere.

An important part of optimism is the belief that everything counts: no person, policy, program, place, or process can be absolutely neutral. Everything that happens in and around schools, and every way it happens add to or take away from successful classroom management. We will explore this notion that everything counts in greater detail later, but for now we will simply affirm that everybody and everything have limitless potential to influence the quality of classroom discipline.

Intentionality

The more intentional a teacher is, the more accurate his or her judgments and the more dependable his or her behavior. The emphasis of Invitational Teaching on intentionality encourages both accuracy and dependability. Moreover, an intentional pattern of teacher behavior leads to purpose, direction, and control of one's personal and professional life.

BE CLEAR. To encourage good discipline, rules should be brief, clear and simple. Give detailed instructions describing the desired procedures. Along with clear rules, provide examples of the specific behaviors expected in this classroom.♪

Cynthia Purkey Norton, daughter of one of the authors, provided an example of the importance of consistent behavior. Cynthia graduated from college in mid-year and accepted an interim teaching position in an inner city school. Unfortunately, the class she inherited had lost several teachers during the year for various reasons. The result was that the class had become very difficult to manage. Cynthia struggled, with only mixed success, to be an Invitational Teacher. While most of the students responded well, one unhappy and sullen girl (we will call her "Judy") showed no improvement. She continued to cause trouble and took great vocal offense at the slightest affront, real or imagined. Cynthia tried hard, but her frequent complaint at the end of a school day was "Dad, it's not working with Judy!" In spite of the lack of success, Cynthia continued to work with Judy in an intentionally caring and appropriate manner. The payoff took place on the final day of school. Judy arrived with a special gift she had laboriously made and inscribed to her "Favorite Teacher." They shared a big hug and a few tears.

It takes a great deal of intentionality to consistently offer something beneficial in the face of apparent failure. How many times does a teacher invite? As long as the heart can endure. With Invitational Teaching, the principles of respect, trust, optimism, and intentionality provide a solid theoretical framework that ties together seemingly unrelated processes embedded within the culture of the school.

The experiences of one of the authors with a student named Keith illustrates how these principles come together. Keith was a student "whose reputation preceded him" to the middle school. His elementary teachers passed along horror stories of his escapades: the day he inked his hands to leave a trail of blue prints along the white walls of his third grade classroom, the time in fourth grade when he used his scissors to "trim" the hair of a girl seated in front of him, his record number of trips to the principal's office in fifth grade. According to records, his previous teachers had tried everything from conferring, consulting, and confronting, to detention, demerits, and deterrents – all to no avail.

When the sixth grade teacher learned that Keith would be one of his students in the fall, he began to plan for success during the summer. Several weeks before the start of the new school year he sent a card to all of his incoming students (including a special note to Keith) welcoming them to his class. Next, he studied Keith's records and found not only an abundance of referrals but also a number of indications of academic potential.

EXPLAIN WHY. Place a simple explanation under each sign to explain why the rule is important. For example, "Please walk" (to ensure everyone's safety). "Please speak softly" (to keep the noise level down). Giving reasons for rules encourages students to follow them.♪

On the first day of class, students were asked to complete autobiographical inventories describing their interests. Keith listed "pets" and "reading" among his "likes." When Keith interrupted class discussion with "Hey, did you hear about the guy who tried to dry his cat in a microwave?" the teacher waved off his comment and moved closer to him. The teacher greeted a second disruption with "Let's talk after class." During their private conference the teacher explained his expectations for the class and asked Keith to talk about his expectations as well. The teacher also asked Keith to help him set up a class aquarium. After the aquarium was operating, the teacher encouraged Keith to join several other students as tutors in a reading program for younger students. Maintaining the aquarium and serving as a tutor helped Keith feel a part of the class and helped him improve his behavior.

In the situation with Keith the invitational stance is visible. The teacher *trusted* Keith to assume responsibility, created an *intentional* plan of action, developed a relationship based on respect, and was *optimistic* that Keith could learn self-discipline and be a successful member of the class. In some happy situations, an Invitational Teacher can overcome a lifetime of unruly behavior.

Up to this point our opening chapter has presented the guiding principles of Invitational Teaching. *Respect* shows in

> *BE A NAMEDROPPER. When necessary to focus a student's attention on the lesson, use his or her name in the context of the lesson. For example, "Charlie, do you think that the author had this in mind?" or "Latoya, tell the class how you think the heroine felt." This strategy encourages students to keep their attention on the lesson content.* ♪

everything the teacher does, including relationships with oneself and others, personally and professionally. *Trust* is manifested by giving students the opportunity to make decisions and create guidelines for accepting responsibility for their own behavior. *Optimism* occurs when the teacher identifies each student's potential to succeed. *Intentionality* maintains consistency in purpose and direction even when it is very difficult to do so.

Such terms as respect, trust, optimism, and intentionality can be so many abstract words until they become alive. To give these terms a human face, we now introduce the "blue and orange card" metaphor.

A Blue and Orange Card Metaphor for Invitational Teaching

I see trees of green, and skies of blue,
They're really people saying I love you.
And I say to myself, what a wonderful world.

Oscar Hamerstein, II
It's A Wonderful World, 1931

Throughout history, metaphors have been used to allow people to think in fresh ways and to create new paradigms. We introduce the "blue and orange card" metaphor here to communicate the deeper meaning of Invitational Teaching. This metaphor allows us to paint a picture of a concept and to highlight the significance of an idea. It also helps the reader to relate to Invitational Teaching at both the intellectual and emotional level.

Before we begin our metaphor it may be useful to point out that metaphors are not absolutely true or accurate pictures. Rather, they provide a pictorial analogy that communicates the significance of a concept. Metaphors are not the product of scientific research and quantitative studies. They are developed by individuals to facilitate understanding and to reduce complex formulations to simple ideas. We create metaphors when we have a desire to communicate ideas that are largely indefinable. Metaphors are useful when there are no concrete or literal terms to describe the concepts behind them. Sam Keen in *The Passionate Life* (1983) described metaphors this way:

> All maps of human life are composed of metaphors. All metaphors are revelatory and inaccurate. To profit by another's experiences, we must become adept at the art of playing with metaphor, translating images, listening for the meaning beneath the nonsense of just-so stories or myths. Consciousness is poetry. We mix our metaphors in order to avoid orthodoxy, literalism, and tyranny. (p. 32)

Studies in semantics (Bateson, 1987; Hayakawa, 1990), psychology (Beck, 1988) and professional counseling

(Gladding, 1992; Purkey & Gerber, 1998) have demonstrated the value and significance of metaphor in communicating symbolic processes. Our blue and orange card metaphor is a highly simplistic explanation of the "signal systems" that exist in every human interaction. These signal systems are both verbal and non-verbal, concrete and abstract, and involve the "Five Powerful P's" to be presented in Chapter Three.

Our metaphor is designed to provide a guide for the symbolic meanings that take place in and around educational settings. Although our focus is on classrooms and schools, our metaphor is useful in many settings, including the home and community.

The card filing system

With remarkably few exceptions, each person born is equipped with a magnificent "card-filing" system called the brain. This tiny, slightly alkaline device runs on glucose and oxygen and contains around a hundred billion logical elements called neurons. The entire system weighs less than three pounds. In a lifetime its data storage capacity can handle 2.78 times ten to the 20th power bits of information. Imagine these myriad bits of information as messages being written on data cards. If each card were the

SHUFFLE THE DECK. Rather than relying on hand-raising or random selection of students, prepare a 3 X 5 card with each student's name. At the beginning of a discussion, shuffle the deck. Call on the student listed on the top card, then place it on the bottom of the deck (or shuffle the deck) and continue to call on everyone in a systematic manner. This eliminates a great deal of hand waving and gives everyone an equal chance of participating.♪

size and weight of a dollar bill, 20 billion would weigh 80,000 tons. Stacked on top of each other, 20 billion cards, each with the thickness of a dollar bill, would stretch 5,428 miles into space. *This is the mental storage capacity of an average person in an average lifetime.* Nothing on earth has more awesome power than the human brain. Teachers who proclaim that a child "does not have the ability" surely lack understanding of the miraculous nature of the human brain.

In highly simplistic terms, as soon as a child is born he or she begins the lifelong task of entering bits of data on cards and storing these cards in his or her mental filing system. Countless cards, each containing a bit of information, are sorted and filed in the brain. The ever-increasing store of cards organizes perceptions and informs the emerging child what the world is like and how things fit together.

Blue and orange cards

In the marvelous card collection process there are only two kinds of cards, blue cards and orange cards. The color represents pure feeling. No matter what bit of information is placed on a card, the card itself is either blue or orange. What is written on a card represents *content* (the lyrics); the color of the card represents the *context* (the melody). We chose the colors "blue" and "orange" in an arbitrary fashion. The colors do not mean anything in and of themselves. We are describing "bluer" than blue and an "oranger" than orange. We present them as metaphors for positive and negative signal systems that exist in every school and that influence classroom discipline.

Blue cards. Blue cards carry a positive feeling that the person is able, valuable, and responsible. They encourage the individual to see the world as a good place to be, where there are many things to love that will love in return. Regardless of content, the context of each blue card encourages the best in self-esteem, excitement for living, and the finest qualities of trust, respect, optimism, and intentionality. Orange cards are exactly the opposite.

Orange cards. Orange cards project feelings that inform the individual that he or she is unable, worthless, and irresponsible. An orange card warns the person to be aware: beware of one's own feelings, of relationships, of life. Orange cards are so painful that individuals will do almost anything to escape the hurt. A major power of drugs and alcohol is that they seem to turn orange to blue, but the effect is illusionary; they only camouflage the pain.

The blue and orange colors for the cards were not chosen to honor or demean an athletic team or to suggest the office fabric be replaced. Blue comes in every color, orange comes in every color. Each time a person is intentionally caring, respecting, trusting, and optimistic, he or she is dealing blue cards. Conversely, each time a person is racist, sexist, homophobic, ethnocentric, insulting, humiliating, uncaring, or thoughtless with oneself or others, personally or professionally, he or she is dealing orange cards.

The 12 to 1 ratio.

In our estimation, each person requires at least 12 blue cards for every one orange card just "to make it through the night." (Our colleague, David Aspy, claims that the ratio is more like 19-1.) These approximate ratios indicate the strength of orange cards and the actions needed to counteract them. When too few blue cards are received, or too many

> *MAKE NO-CUT CONTRACTS. Explain to students the long-lasting effects of racist, sexist, or other negative orange card comments. Ask them to make a "no-cut" contract to include all students and the teacher: "In this classroom I will not put myself down, I will not put you down. You will not put yourself down, you will not put me down." If a student or teacher breaks the contract, he or she can be gently but firmly reminded by everyone of the commitment.* ♪

orange, the ratio falls "below minimum" and terrible things begin to happen. Individuals begin to lose self-esteem, optimism, and hope. This loss is coupled with the appearance of pessimism, hostility, and anger. "Nobody likes me, or respects me or cares about me, so I don't like, respect, or care about others either." "If I can't be the best, I'll be the best at being the worst." Thus, the classroom misbehavior generates its own negative energy.

A matter of life or death

It will be helpful to pause here and contemplate the deeper meaning of the blue and orange card metaphor. It's not about being "nice," providing "warm fuzzies," giving "strokes," forming "hug stations," distributing bumper stickers, or walking around with "IALAC" (I am lovable and capable) posters. While these are usually worthwhile activities when used caringly and appropriately, they are insufficient to describe the awesome nature and potential power of each and every card. Sticks and stones break bones, orange cards kill.

Often it is temptingly easy for a teacher to go orange – to "let people have it – tell them off – give them a piece of one's mind." Such orange behavior is usually counterproductive. It

KEEP IT CLEAN. Research studies (Gladwell, 2000) suggest that when teachers and students work together to keep the classroom and school neat and clean, the amount of graffiti and vandalism is reduced significantly and student conduct is improved.♪

may be more difficult to go blue, but it is more beneficial. Those who receive blue cards are most likely to continue the process. The reason the blue and orange card metaphor is valuable is that it serves as a constant reminder that everything people do and every way they do it is either positive or negative, beneficial or lethal, inviting or disinviting.

As documented elsewhere (Purkey & Schmidt, 1987; Purkey & Stanley, 1991; Purkey, 2000; Purkey & Siegel, 2002), everything counts. The way a phone is answered, a letter written, a word spoken, an office painted, a colleague treated, a policy established, a program implemented is either helpful or harmful. *Everything adds to, or subtracts from, positive classroom discipline.* Because this is so, those with wish to deal in blue cards carefully monitor the quality of programs, places, processes, policies, and the nature of every human interaction.

Maslow (1970) captured the essence of the blue and orange card metaphor when he wrote

> Let people clearly realize that every time they threaten someone or humiliate or hurt unnecessarily or dominate or reject another human being, they become forces for the creation of psychopathology, even if these be small forces. Let them recognize that every

> man (sic) who is kind, helpful, decent, psychologically democratic, affectionate, and warm, is a psychotherapeutic force even though a small one. (p. 254)

It is increasingly clear that everything we do and every way we do it is either orange or blue. Nothing is neutral.

Summary

Invitational Teachers make choices in everything they do. The blue cards they give to themselves and others, personally and professionally, may not be enough to outweigh the orange, but each one counts. Therefore, it is vital that the Invitational Teacher mentally "color codes" everything in the school – either blue or orange. Invitational Teachers have a responsibility to share their vision of the school – to find ways to communicate what may be possible when everyone works together. Communication of this vision can be enhanced by use of the blue and orange card metaphor.

> *TURN ORANGE TO BLUE. When a student has acted in an unacceptable way, try this approach: say: "I know you can behave better than this." Point out the correct way of behaving; "Talk quietly, so you won't disturb others," then say: "This is the way I want you to behave. Will you please do this for me?" This encourages clear communication, cooperation, and student responsibility.* ♪

Just as scientists from every discipline use metaphors to describe concepts and events for which there are no literal terms, Invitational Teachers use the blue and orange metaphor in sharing a vision. The emotional impact of a metaphor can provide impetus for people in organizations to try new ideas and fresh approaches. The blue and orange card metaphor is one way Invitational Teaching can be understood and communicated in a vivid and colorful way.

This opening chapter has introduced the concept of Invitational Teaching, with its guiding principles of respect, trust, optimism, and intentionality. These principles are manifested in our blue and orange card metaphor. Chapter Two will use this metaphor to look at the classroom. ♫

2.

WHAT COLOR IS YOUR CLASSROOM?

Creating and maintaining a productive classroom environment has been, and probably always will be, a major challenge to teachers. Early approaches to classroom management were primarily punitive. One of the first schoolhouses built in the United States was equipped with a whipping post (Manning, 1959), and throughout history all sorts of techniques were used to inflict physical and psychological punishment on students as a means of keeping order in the classroom.

Although vestiges of a more punitive and primitive time in North American history still linger in many schools (use of ridicule, public humiliation, corporal punishment, assertive discipline, etc.) most contemporary methods of maintaining discipline are positive and humane. However, many disinviting "orange" processes that contribute to poor discipline still remain in schools.

This chapter presents four levels of personal and professional functioning and demonstrates how each of the four levels detracts from, or adds to, good classroom discipline. The four levels are *intentionally orange, unintentionally orange, unintentionally blue* and *intentionally blue.*

Level One: Intentionally Orange

The most toxic and lethal level of personal and professional functioning has been described as "intentionally disinviting" (Purkey & Novak, 1996). This bottom level of functioning can take place in one or more of five dimensions found in any school. These dimensions will be presented later in this monograph as the "Five P's" (people, places, policies, programs, processes).

Intentionally disinviting practices are those specifically designed to demean, dissuade, discourage, and defeat. Examples of Level I, intentionally orange functioning might be seen in *people* (deliberate racial, sexual, or ethnic insults), *places* (willfully left dirty or squalid), *policies* (specifically harassing or elitist), *programs* (purposefully biased and discriminatory), and *processes* (deliberately cruel and disrespectful). Whether found separately or collectively, such negative forces in these five areas can only be defined as intentionally disinviting.

Unfortunately, a few teachers resemble Elmira Gulch in the 1939 film version of L. F. Baum's *Wizard of Oz.* Like Elmira, they take pleasure in hurting people or seeing them upset. As one administrator bragged; "I don't have ulcers, I give them." In our opinion, educators who function at the intentionally disinviting level should seek other employment or obtain professional counseling. Their deliberate negative signals may be understandable, even forgivable, but not justifiable. In Invitational Teaching, intentionally disinviting places, policies, programs, and processes cannot be justified regardless of effectiveness or efficiency. There is no justification, particularly for those who aspire to be Invitational Teachers, to remain at the intentionally disinviting level.

As we explained in Chapter One, Invitational Teaching centers on optimism, trust, respect, and intentionality. When teachers abandon this center and rely on ridicule, sarcasm, and force, students are likely to respond in kind. It is sad but true that there are still a few educators who spend part of their energies in creating and maintaining intentionally "orange" environments. Such faculty and staff take a certain relish in being rude to each other, to students, to parents, and to visitors. The physical plant is a mess, the policies are dictatorial, the programs are sexist, racist, and biased; and the processes are uncaring and often capricious.

A glaring example of Level I Functioning was described to one of the authors by a middle school teacher who entered the girls' restroom at her school and noticed that there were no soap or towels. She wrote a note to the principal requesting soap and towels for the restrooms. The principal sent the note back with this question scribbled across the bottom: "What do you think this is, the Hilton?" Whether because of racial prejudice, sadistic impulse, basic distrust, or whatever, a few schools seem to function at Level I. But whatever the cause, *there is no justification for people, places, policies, programs, or processes to function at the intentionally disinviting level.* Schools that languish at Level I should seek intensive inservice training in Invitational Education for the entire faculty and staff. After all, who would want to be an orange teacher in an orange school?

This intentionally disinviting bottom level may be thought of as "lethal orange" functioning. Lethal orange functioning occurs in at least two ways. The first happens when a person becomes angry and frustrated and makes a decision based on these feelings. Examples might be a judge who orders juvenile offenders to be locked up with hardened criminals to "teach them a lesson," a father who loses his temper and strikes his child, an administrator who publicly berates a secretary, or a teacher who shoves a student. There is great danger in the willingness of some to legitimize intentionally disinviting actions.

A second way that lethal orange functioning occurs is when individuals use their positions of power to behave unethically, illegally, or immorally, for example, the principal who attempts to seduce an employee, the prejudiced school counselor who repeatedly discourages certain students from applying for college, or a teacher who dislikes certain groups, such as athletes or cheerleaders, and grades them unfairly.

A classic example of lethal functioning may be seen in the play *Amadeus*. Salieri, consumed by professional jealousy, sets out with murderous intent to destroy Mozart. Salieri discovered Mozart's greatest fear and used this knowledge with deadly effect. It is sad to note that there are some people who have a certain lethal talent for sending intentionally disinviting messages to others regarding their value, abilities, or competencies.

USE COMMON SENSE. Nothing will take the place of good judgment in maintaining good discipline. If a behavior is considered unacceptable one day, it is unacceptable on other days. Moreover, don't make threats or assign penalties that cannot be carried out. ♪

A further example of lethal functioning was shared by one of our friends, a female principal, who decided to go back to school and earn her Ph.D. When she approached the university faculty advisor and expressed her desire to enroll in the doctoral program, she was told to forget this idea, that she was not "marketable." At a meeting some weeks later, she shared what had transpired with two of her female colleagues. The two women principals told her that they, too, had the desire to earn a doctorate and had talked with this same faculty advisor. They, too, had been discouraged from entering a doctoral program. As they talked, a male principal joined the conversation. He said that he had met with the same professor, and that he had been *encouraged* to enroll. It appears that this faculty advisor was a serial killer of female aspirations.

Being human, teachers may slip into disinviting modes of functioning on occasion. We are, after all, human beings first and teachers second. Thankfully, most teachers who function at a disinviting level do so unintentionally, which brings us to the second level of orange functioning.

Level Two: Unintentionally Orange

People in schools that typically function at the unintentionally disinviting orange level often ask themselves such questions as: "Why are people in this school so unfriendly?" "What makes this school so depressing?" "Why are our policies, programs, and processes not working?" "Why are the students so unruly?" The answers may lie in Level II orange functioning. The people, places, policies, programs, and processes that make up the school are unintentionally disinviting.

Teachers who create and maintain unintentionally disinviting orange classrooms are usually well-meaning and high-minded, but the behaviors they exhibit, the environments they create, the policies, programs and processes they introduce are often uncaring, unsightly, inappropriate, and unfair. Disinviting messages can last for a surprisingly long time.

Examples of unintentionally disinviting processes appear often in student descriptions of their school experiences. "My last name is Burkey," commented one student, "and the teacher always called me 'Turkey' and laughed. I think the teacher meant well, but she never realized how much she embarrassed me in front of the class." Another student described her frustration over a teacher who asked her "Would you rather that I refer to you as Black or African American?" "I just wish she would refer to me as Joanne."

Countless factors and variables influence teachers' daily activities. Interruptions from important work, pressures to attend meetings and complete tasks, demands from supervisors and principals, overdue projects, personnel conflicts, physical ailments, noise levels, even the temperature, weather, or time of day, week, or month can influence both the degree of intentionality and level of functioning. At such times these myriad demands and factors can be such that teachers act or react in ways that are perceived by others as disinviting even though this was not intended.

GET THERE EARLY. There are countless causes of tension and anxiety that are unavoidable, but one major cause of teacher tension is cutting time too short and running behind. Make a vow to set the alarm a little earlier, go to bed earlier, and arrive at school relaxed, calm, and collected. Your day will go much better when you get off to a good start. ♪

Illustrations of unintentionally disinviting orange behaviors are: continuing to work at one's desk with eyes down while someone stands there waiting to be recognized, drinking coffee during class without offering students something to drink, giving a finger-crunching handshake, answering a phone in the middle of a conversation, telling inappropriate jokes, or even arranging office furniture so that the teacher has a "throne" while visitors are seated in small, straight-backed chairs.

Sometimes orange actions are caused by misdirected attempts to impress visitors with one's authority and power. However, the most likely cause is a simple lack of sensitivity, politeness, and good manners. For this reason, civility, common courtesies, proper manners, and sensitivity to appearance are given high priority in Invitational Teaching. Life is never so hurried or busy that the teacher has no time for politeness and common courtesy.

Orange humor

Sometimes, attempts at humor can be unintentionally disinviting. What is meant to be funny can come across as mocking and even cruel. Consider these comments posted to walls or placed on desks:

"You have obviously mistaken me for someone who cares."

"Have a nice day, somewhere else."

"What part of NO don't you understand?"

"The next time you're passing by, keep going."

"Abandon hope all ye who enter here."

"Come on in, everything else has gone wrong today."

"I'd like to help you out, which way did you come in?"

While usually meant to be funny, comments like the above can be unintentionally disinviting.

Orange labeling

A major cause of student unhappiness and misbehavior is the tendency of many schools to develop policies, programs, and processes that focus on groups of students as being "different." When teachers begin to think in terms of "learning disabled," "culturally disadvantaged," "at risk," "emotionally disturbed," or "troublemaker," instead of thinking of each student as a unique human being, there is the danger that the concept of "different" itself may cause student misbehavior. Viewing certain groups of students as different may unintentionally elicit student feelings of inferiority, resentment, and hostility. This self-fulfilling circle closes when students who have been labeled in negative ways accept the label and begin to behave accordingly. *Students tend to live up or down to the expectations of significant people in their lives.*

The unhappy result of people, places, policies, programs and processes functioning at the orange level (I or II) is that many students are more disinvited than they are disadvantaged, disabled, or undisciplined. And whether the impact of disinviting experiences is intentional or unintentional, the negative results are usually the same.

Orange actions

An incident that illustrates inappropriate and uncaring behavior happened to one of the authors when he was invited to keynote a large teacher convention. Following the keynote address, all the participants headed for small-group workshops. I approached the conference registration area and asked the person behind the desk where I might get a cup of coffee. The person responded by asking abruptly, "What workshop are you with?" I explained that I was not with a workshop, to which the person responded "Coffee is served at 10:30, you'll have to wait." At that moment, a custodian walked by and said to me: "There's a coffee shop on the second floor and I'm going that way. I'll show you where it is." The custodian was demonstrating caring and appropriate behavior, which cannot be said of the person behind the desk who was, at best, unintentionally disinviting.

SHARE THE GLORY. Create and support a school policy that class officers, school cheerleaders, and students selected for responsibilities should be selected to represent as many students as possible. Creating an "out" group is a sure way to elicit student hostility, misbehavior, and even violence.♪

Like those at the intentionally disinviting bottom level, teachers who function at the unintentionally disinviting level may experience positive results from time to time. This is not too surprising. People are helped in all sorts of ways, sometimes in spite of disinviting orange actions. As the fictional detective Charlie Chan noted "Strange events permit themselves the luxury of occurring." However, when positive results occur regularly, it is a good bet that the teacher is functioning at an inviting "blue level," either unintentionally or intentionally.

Level Three: Unintentionally Blue

Teachers who are unintentionally inviting are often successful in maintaining good classroom discipline, but they rarely know why. They behave as they do through trial and error, guesswork, or intuition. But because they have no clear understanding of the dynamics that contribute to success, they often lack consistency in direction. They can be trustful as long as they have no reason to distrust. They can be purposeful as long as what is needed is obvious. They can be respectful as long as they are treated with respect, and they are optimistic only so long as things go well. Simply stated, teachers who function at the unintentionally inviting level know what they are doing, but they do not know *why.* When these teachers encounter discipline problems they have difficulty in figuring out why the problems are occurring or how to handle them. Of greater concern, when faced with difficult and demanding challenges (such as disrespectful or disruptive student behavior) teachers who function at Blue Level III are likely to resort to Orange Level II, or even Orange Level I functioning. Because these unintentionally inviting teachers are unaware of the causes of their successes or failures, they tend to be inconsistent. They have no unifying theory of practice on which to anchor their discipline efforts.

Many teachers who function at the unintentionally inviting Blue Level have the personal qualities that contribute to successful teaching. They are sometimes referred to as "natural-born" teachers. They are usually optimistic, respectful, and trusting. *Yet the one critical quality they lack is intentionality.* When one teacher was exposed to Invitational Teaching, he exclaimed, "I've been doing this for years, but I didn't know why I was doing it." Because some teachers lack intentionality, they are likely to be inconsistent in their work and unpredictable in their actions. The lack of consistency jeopardizes their ability to become an Invitational Teacher.

As an analogy, teachers who function at the unintentionally inviting level resemble the early "barn-storming" airplane pilots. These pioneer aviators did not know much about aerodynamics, weather patterns, or global navigation or positioning systems. As long as they stayed close to the ground, where they could follow railway lines or highways, and the weather remained favorable, they did fine. But when night fell or the weather turned ugly, they could easily become disoriented and lost. In challenging situations they lacked consistency in direction. Attempting to practice Invitational Teaching without an explicit theoretical rationale is like flying a plane without a compass, preparing dinner without a plan, or driving at night without headlights.

The basic problem with unintentionally inviting blue functioning is that the teacher can become disoriented and unable to identify the reasons for his or her successes or failures. If whatever "it" is should stop working, the teacher does not know how to start it up again or what changes to make. (In baseball, this is known as a "slump.") In these situations, the teacher lacks a consistent stance – a dependable position from which to operate. When the teacher is unintentionally inviting, his or her credibility is at risk. He or she depends too often on serendipitous teaching.

MAKE YOUR FLIGHT PLAN. One of the precautions pilots take before taking off is to check flight plans. Successful teachers have their own checklists before teaching. Some items might be:

√ Will this activity work with these students?

√ Are all the materials ready?

√ Will the directions be understandable?

√ Are the transitions between activities smooth and clear?

√ Is this the best time to do this activity? Avoiding the appearance of confusion is a good way to avoid student misbehavior. ♪

Serendipitous teaching

The word serendipity comes from an old Persian folk tale describing the antics of the three princes of Serendip. Although they were shrewd and discerning, they relied on chance. Because teachers who typically function at the unintentionally inviting blue level have personal qualities and strengths that are conducive to successful teaching, they are often considered capable. They know *what* they are doing, but not *why.* This lack of understanding is a serious barrier to exploiting their potential as teachers. It also places students at risk, since the teacher's approach tends to be trial and error. The teacher's success is not a product of intentionality, but rather a matter of serendipity or, to put it bluntly, pure chance.

One additional analogy may be helpful. Teachers who function at the unintentionally inviting level are like amateurs who enjoy looking for Indian arrowheads. They know what to look for, and they may discover an arrowhead or two, but their luck is no match for the professional archaeologist who knows where, when, how, and what to look for in seeking relics. The archaeologist of Invitational Teaching is the one who knows when, where, how, and why to be intentionally inviting with oneself and others, personally and professionally.

It should be noted at this point that the concept of Invitational Teaching presented here is much easier to apply when things are going well and when discipline is not a problem. But a hallmark of Invitational Teaching is to function well in difficult situations. After all, anyone can be inviting when the sun is shining and no one is ruffling one's feathers. The true test of the Invitational Teacher is creating and maintaining a consistently inviting stance, even in the rain, which brings us to the top level of professional functioning: intentionally blue.

Level Four: Intentionally Blue

Intentionality allows Invitational Teachers to achieve direction, purpose, and skill in their actions. It is through intentionality that they are able to choose appropriate and caring strategies and to behave accordingly. In times of turbulence, the teacher who is functioning at the intentionally inviting blue level is like a command pilot of a large jet airliner. Thanks to their specialized knowledge, these pilots can "fly on instruments" around and over dangerous weather fronts. This ability to chart and maintain a dependable flight pattern spells the difference between their success and failure in reaching their destination in a safe and desirable manner.

ESTABLISH A ROUTINE. Have a systematic routine for all classroom procedures. By creating and maintaining an established way of involving students in administering classroom routine (distributing materials, listing the agenda on the board, preparing the audiovisual, collecting assignments), teachers improve classroom discipline and use time effectively.♪

The ability to maintain a consistent and desirable stance is important in both personal and professional functioning. Consistency moves the teacher beyond the reality of technological proficiency toward a quality of character based as much on who he or she is as what he or she knows. Invitational Teachers are living examples of their guiding principles of optimism, trust, respect, and intentionality. By serving as role models, they demonstrate desirable behavior.

It should be noted here that being intentionally inviting requires a certain measure of courage and bravery. By definition, an Invitational Teacher is one who breaks new ground. Without the courage to act, the teacher becomes simply a participant or functionary, providing service but little or no inspiration.

Teachers who have reached the intentionally inviting blue level have a special style. This style is revealed through the teacher's vision, values, hopes, aspirations, and beliefs. He or she is able to perform with such skill and grace that the art is invisible to all but the trained observer. As the Fox explains in de Saint-Exupéry's (1943) *The Little Prince:* "And now here is my secret, a very simple secret: It is only with the heart that one can see rightly; what is essential is invisible to the eye" (p. 87).

At this point the reader might be asking: "What about the students who insist on misbehaving, even in the most intentionally inviting environment?" It is true that there will always be students who violate the most reasonable and appropriate rules. Students are not robots. (Even in heaven there were discipline problems. Lucifer, light-filled, Son of the Morning, had to be expelled.) There are those few students who will repeatedly resist control and who will cause disruption.

When disruption does occur, the teacher who functions at Level IV (Intentionally Blue) will ask such questions as these: "Are our rules reasonable, fair, and enforceable?" (Sometimes an unreasonable, unfair, or largely unenforceable rule, such as "no gum in school" or "no talking during lunch" will trigger discipline problems). Are there disinviting factors at work (e.g., rude or thoughtless actions, unpleasant processes, dictatorial policies, ruthless academic competitions, peer isolation) that are contributing to the discipline problem? Does the misbehaving student need professional counseling? (The student's misbehavior may have *nothing to do* with the school's people, places, policies, programs, or processes). If questions such as these are answered to the teacher's satisfaction and the misbehavior is still unexcused, an appropriate consequence is necessary, which brings us to the subject of penalties and punishments.

Even in light of the harshest realities and most difficult situations, teachers who strive to operate at the intentionally inviting blue level work to maintain an inviting stance. These teachers avoid reliance on corporal punishment or psychological warfare. Penalties for misbehavior are used sparingly and are applied with an attitude of respect for the offender and sadness at the offense. Invitational Teachers understand the differences between a state trooper and a storm trooper. They point out the logical connection between the misbehavior and the consequence. Penalties (in the form of loss of privileges) should not give students the resentful feeling of being wronged. Consequences are designed to encourage students to reflect on the offense, recognize why the offense was uncaring or inappropriate, and discover what they can do to conduct themselves better in the future. When unavoidable, penalties should instruct students, not depreciate them.

TAKE A STRETCH BREAK. If students become fidgety or restless during class, take a one-minute stretch break where everyone stands and does a few simple bending and stretching exercises. Even the game "Simon Says" can enliven a classroom so that misbehavior caused by boredom or restlessness is minimized or eliminated ♪

Summary

This chapter has presented Invitational Teaching in terms of four levels of professional functioning. Level I, intentionally disinviting, is the province of those forces in and around schools that deliberately demean, discourage, and dissuade students. Level II, unintentionally disinviting, is the domain of those thoughtless forces that are well-meaning but are uncaring and inappropriate. While these Level II forces are usually unwitting, they can be just as lethal and toxic as the bottom level. Level III, unintentionally inviting, is the province of the teacher. He or she is often able to create good classroom discipline but cannot explain why things go well. When things stop working, the natural born teacher may resort to lower levels of functioning. The fourth level of functioning, intentionally inviting, is the high level of performance by teachers that is most likely to result in positive classroom discipline and productive learning.

Traditionally, the creation and maintenance of good student discipline has relied on establishing rules, targeting misbehaviors, and exacting penalties. In contrast, this chapter has promoted the belief that Invitational Teaching, with its stance of optimism, trust, respect, and intentionality is the surest and most enlightened approach to invite positive classroom discipline while promoting academic achievement. Our very best teachers, the ones considered experts by their peers, demonstrate this stance in consistent and inspiring ways. Understanding this stance may help teachers in the early stages of their careers gain this expertise. In the next chapter, we show how the whole school environment can nurture and support this inviting blue stance. ♫

3.

THE FIVE POWERFUL *P's*: CREATING SCHOOL CULTURES THAT PROMOTE SELF-DISCIPLINE

Good classroom discipline is no accident. It is the intended product of people, places, policies, programs, and processes working together. Based on our studies of successful practices, we have discovered that Invitational Teaching requires not only great skill, but also great heart. Creating meaningful personal and academic connections with students is a blending of art and science, compelled by a commitment to provide the optimistic, respectful, and trusting stance that Invitational Teachers intentionally develop.

Many teachers manage to put "blue card" dynamics in motion in classrooms that are surrounded by less inviting school climates. These "islands in the stream" provide a safe haven for students and serve as testimony to the persistently inviting actions of their teachers. Invitational Teaching is even more powerful when it occurs in a welcoming school culture that promotes caring. In this chapter, we summarize our studies of school culture and offer suggestions for strengthening the impact of Invitational Teaching through collaboration.

Since the publication of *Positive Discipline: A Pocketful of Ideas* in 1986, a forerunner to this volume, we have been studying successful school reform (Strahan, 1994; Purkey & Strahan, 1995; L'Esperance, Strahan, & Farrington, 2001).

While the dynamics of school change vary according to the particular context of the school, the primary feature of success is the improvement in school culture. Wolcott (1999) defines culture as the ways people go about their lives and the belief systems associated with their behavior (p. 25). The essence of school culture is a shared sense of "who we are and how we do things around here" (Strahan, 1994, p. 7). Improving a school culture requires a clear understanding of the ways that everything is connected. We refer to this at the Jell-O principle.

The Jell-O principle provides a powerful framework for school improvement. When attempting to improve discipline, everything matters. Culture is the "gel" in the Jell-0. Like great Jell-O dishes, each school may have a unique blend of ingredients and flavor. What binds the ingredients together is the "gel" of shared beliefs about what matters and shared ways of doing things to accomplish these priorities. In the very best schools, the culture promotes "significance." These schools are guided by moral purpose – to make a positive and significant difference in the lives of students, families, and communities. These schools are more than successful, they are significant. Students and

> *THE JELL-O PRINCIPLE. The school and everybody in it is like one big bowl of Jell-O: if you touch it anywhere, the whole thing jiggles; everything is connected to everything else. Understanding the Jell-o principle helps the teacher to remember that everything: temperature, time of day, color of walls, how the teacher dresses, adds to or subtracts from positive classroom discipline. No effort to make the school more inviting is wasted.*♪

teachers not only achieve academically, they become better people. Transforming schools from mediocre to successful, and from successful to significant, requires a strengthening of the gel itself. It requires a concerted effort to enhance all of the aspects of culture.

It is difficult, yet vital, to assess the impact of cultural dynamics in an empirical fashion. In one of the most productive efforts to measure a school culture, Miller and Hoy (2000) designed a set of instruments to measure teachers' perceptions of school culture. They then examined student achievement in relationship to these indicators. They based their study on the theoretical construct of "a culture of openness" which they defined as "characterized by shared identity, openness, authenticity, trust, cooperation, and shared decision making" (p. 52). They developed assessments for each of these factors and administered them to 2741 teachers from 86 middle schools in New Jersey. Next, they compared the ratings of cultural factors with data regarding student achievement and school organization. Results showed that a culture of openness promoted student achievement and organizational effectiveness in significant ways (pp. 59-60). Their quantitative study supports the findings of our longitudinal case studies that "teachers become more student-centered and students become more responsive when everyone feels valuable, able, and responsible; when adults in the school are committed to providing personal support for students; when teachers and administrators become advocates for students; and when everyone feels part of a team" (Strahan, 1994, p. 10).

To guide efforts toward school improvement, Invitational Education (Purkey & Novak, 1996) provides a framework that focuses on five essential aspects of education. These "five powerful P's" are people, places, policies, programs, and processes. In applying this framework to good discipline it is necessary to look beyond teachers and students (the "people") to take into account places, policies, programs and processes. The secret of good discipline lies in combining all of these factors into a consistently productive and caring environment. A consideration of each of these five major factors follows.

People

Authorities on classroom management agree that the relationship between teacher and student is the most critical factor in establishing good discipline in the classroom (Jones, 1996; Good & Brophy, 2000). Several reports have described recurring patterns of beliefs and behaviors among teachers who are successful in establishing positive environments for learning.

In one of the most comprehensive studies of the relationships between school context and adolescent development, Roeser, Eccles, and Sameroff (2000) examined data collected from more than 800 seventh and eighth grade students across a two-year period. Results showed that students who made the most academic progress and showed the strongest personal growth shared three key convictions:

- They believed that their teachers regarded them positively
- They believed that their teachers gave them emotional support
- They believed that their curricula were meaningful.

Based on these findings, the researchers encouraged teachers and administrators to eliminate school practices that foster excessive competition and to craft lessons that help students connect with their daily lives. They also recommended that schools create smaller communities for learning, examine potential discriminatory practices, and be more proactive in promoting physical and mental health.

The picture that emerges from descriptions of successful teachers is that they tend to be caring, sensitive, active people who understand their students and who find numerous ways to send inviting messages. Though not explicitly stated, these reports suggest an image of Invitational Teachers who express gentle caring and firm expectations simultaneously. As one teacher commented, "Just because I smile a lot doesn't mean I don't expect a lot." Students in classes whose behavior requires correction are "reminded" rather than "reprimanded." The positive messages these teachers send are not haphazard or accidental. As Brophy (1983) concluded, "the seemingly automatic, smooth-functioning routines observable in the classrooms of successful managers result from a great deal of preparation and organization" (p. 269). Such teachers are intentionally providing a blue environment for learning.

TALK WITH STUDENTS. Dialogue is an essential and fulfilling activity for human beings, so try to talk things out. Find out how things seem from the student's point of view. Whenever possible, deal with a misbehaving student privately, on a one-on-one basis. This permits students to avoid feeling "on stage" and may allow them to speak more freely. ♪

In the most successful schools, every person contributes to and benefits from a supportive culture. The "people" aspect of the school includes everyone: students, parents, teachers, community members, guests, bus drivers, librarians, cafeteria workers, nurses, secretaries, home-school coordinators, administrators, and anyone else who has a stake in the school. Positive classroom discipline begins with people.

Places

While teachers and students are the "people" most important to good discipline, the entire "place" of the school is a second essential factor. Visitors to schools have long noted that certain buildings feel "sunny" and welcoming. Other buildings, while perhaps as new and as well furnished, feel "gloomy" and disinviting. While school buildings themselves have not yet been related directly to academic achievement, Johnston's (1985) studies of the climates of successful middle schools documented the importance of the physical environment in students' and teachers' perceptions of their schools. When asked "How do you know the school cares about you and your learning?" students most often suggested that the cleanliness of the school showed them that the school staff "cares" (p. 3).

As a specific example of how places can influence student behavior, consider the nature of the school cafeteria. Some schools we visit seem to have adopted a "prison model" cafeteria. The atmosphere is institutional. The mood is dreary. Lunch lines are long. The walls are painted gray. Students cannot talk to each other. Regardless of the quality of the food, most students (and teachers) seem anxious to escape. Other schools, in contrast, have attractive places for students and teachers to eat. Some schools offer stand-up tables for students who are tired of sitting, colorful walls, and attractive salad bars. Students in these cafeteria settings are more likely to enjoy their lunch and behave themselves.

Our analyses of the dynamics of school transformation in a longitudinal study of school reform indicated that efforts to improve the school grounds provided concrete and tangible measures of change. Improvements such as flower beds, renovated commons areas, and benches for outdoor meetings helped set the stage for more intangible changes in the ways "teachers and students see themselves, each other, and their school" (Purkey & Strahan, 1995, p. 6). As mentioned throughout this book, schools are best measured by the way they invite everyone to feel able, valuable, and responsible. The atmosphere in these inviting places is based on respect and trust rather than on rules and regulations.

PAINT SOME MURALS. Blank walls, hallways, cafeterias, classrooms can be brightened with larger-than-life murals. These murals can be as simple as taping large rolls of white paper on walls, using the opaque projector and a group of students with magic markers, or they can be a cooperative project of the art and social studies teachers. The results give the students pride in their environment and teach them cooperation. Not only are these murals attractive, they also provide tangible evidence that the school values students' contributions. ♪

No matter how old or worn out their facilities or equipment, Invitational Teachers make the best of them to create "places" that promote positive discipline.

Policies

In addition to people and places, policies contribute greatly to the quality of life in classrooms. Policies are everywhere. The federal government establishes policies as do regional, provincial, state, and local agencies. Principals, too, establish policies, and so do classroom teachers. The result is that sometimes policies are instituted without regard for each other or the impact they may have on the total school environment.

USE INVITATIONAL PRINCIPLES. An Invitational Code of Discipline should reflect eight basic principles. It should 1) be consistent with Invitational Teaching, 2) be developed cooperatively with students and parents, 3) respect legal rights, 4) be positively worded and understandable, 5) be reasonable and explain why, 6) be inclusive and non-discriminatory, 7) identify enforceable consequences, and 8) be widely communicated.

A key dimension of policy is the role of "rules" regarding discipline. In their review of research on classroom management, Good and Brophy (2000) emphasized that rules are necessary to define expectations for classroom conduct. "Usually, four or five general rules, suited to the grade level and the instructional goals, are sufficient" and "it is often useful to involve students in these discussions" (p. 128).

It would seem that "rules" themselves do not matter as much as common expectations among students and teachers. (In the Munchkin Land of Oz, there was only one rule that covered everything: "Behave yourself!"). Whether these expectations are written or not, everyone in the school should be able to expect the same standard of respect and decency.

One successful middle school teacher has "one rule that covers everything" – respect. He spends time with students on the first day of class discussing the concept of respect and relates it to disruptions when they occur. He has found that this practice frees him from "rule fixation" and helps students assume responsibility for their own behavior.

People and places are heavily influenced by policies: the regulations, codes, orders, mandates, plans, rules, and edicts created by those responsible for life in schools. But as noted earlier, policies are sometimes created that, while well-intended, place unfair or unreasonable restrictions on teachers and students alike. An example of a counter-productive policy might be a "zero tolerance" position that requires mandatory suspension for certain offenses such as "fighting," "talking back," or "cutting class." Regardless of circumstances, the student who fights, talks back, or skips school is suspended. This seems to suggest a sort of "mindlessness" on the part of school officials. The welfare of students should determine any school policy.

WORK TOGETHER ON POLICIES. In developing policies governing student behavior, it is important to include as many people as possible. Systems of management for hallways, classrooms, entrances, cafeterias and the like can best be developed through collaboration with custodians, food service workers, counselors, students, parents, the principal, and others who have an investment in good discipline. ♪

Attendance policies are also blue or orange. (Suspending students for skipping school is ironic and can easily backfire). Using suspension as a school policy has the unhappy result in that it removes the student from the very place where he or she might learn to behave. It also places the student behind in schoolwork. Any school discipline policy should be made in light of its total impact on the student's life.

Programs

Schools create various curricular and co-curricular programs as part of their offerings. For example, after-school enrichment programs, athletic programs, gifted programs, special education programs, extracurricular programs are all designed to meet the educational goals of the school. But like some school policies that have negative side effects, programs can be counterproductive as well. Some school programs focus on narrow objectives and neglect a wider perspective of student needs.

An example of a program that carries a terrible side effect is the process of "cutting" the athletic squad. In this painful process young boys and girls who would *most* benefit from athletic activity are told that they did not "make the team." Such rejection by highly significant authority figures can have long-term negative consequences. Invitational Teaching calls for educators to consider every aspect of various school programs to ensure that everyone and everything adds to, not detracts from, the original goals for which they were intended.

The Behavior Improvement Program (BIP) at Guilford Middle School in Guilford County, North Carolina, provides an example of a program based on Invitational Education principles that has successfully addressed the needs of students. In the early 1980s, teachers and administrators at Guilford Middle School explored ways to provide students with a more supportive structure for improving their behavior. They examined traditional approaches to "In-School Suspension" and found that most of them emphasized punishment more than development. Often staffed by paraprofessionals or teachers with less-than-full schedules, such programs rarely offered the level of support they wanted. Ms. Helen Stone, a veteran language arts teacher with a strong reputation for working with "unmotivated" students, expressed interest in developing an invitational approach to behavior improvement. She designed the BIP program as an alternative to traditional out-of-school suspension. She noted in the beginning that for the at-risk student, being "sent home" might temporarily meet the needs of the school faculty and staff; however it rarely helped the individual student involved. In fact, to those at risk, these measures are tangible proof that school is not the place for them. They provide strong incentive for dropping out – emotionally and, later perhaps, literally.

Almost 20 years later, Ms. Stone continues to serve as teacher for the Behavior Improvement Program. She has developed a program that enriches and extends the school's academic goals. The central goals of the BIP are to maintain an in-school suspension program that benefits students academically, socially, and personally, and to maintain a disciplined and caring learning environment in which students receive assistance with academic and study skills. As she indicated in her written description of the program, the philosophy of the BIP is that "You made a bad choice, but you're not a bad kid."

The BIP room is near the principal's office and features colorful posters that promote high expectations and personal responsibility. When students arrive, they sit in study carrels that give them workspace and privacy. Students participate in the program in three ways. An administrator can assign them to BIP for one or more days for an infraction that, before the program started, might have resulted in an out-of-school suspension. In some instances, individual students have a behavior contract that specifies time-out sessions in BIP for certain infractions.

The key to success of the program is that Ms. Stone works with students to help them connect the choices they have made with the potential consequences of their behavior. If students enter the room feeling angry, she gives them an opportunity to "vent" by writing about their frustrations. Later, they can trash their paper or file it for future reference. After they have given up some of their anger, Ms. Stone talks with them in a non-threatening fashion, encouraging them to identify the decisions they made that resulted in the assignment to BIP. While in BIP, students work on assignments for the classes they are missing. Ms. Stone keeps a large file of teaching resources on hand to assist them with their work. She involves teachers, parents, and the students themselves in designing plans for improving behavior. She notes that "being isolated from the mainstream of peers, classes, and activities is by nature a negative, punitive consequence. However, while the student is in BIP, there is much potential for positive academic and personal skills and attitudes to develop."

One of the authors who has visited the BIP often has observed that students appreciate Ms. Stone's efforts on their behalf. During class changes, many stop by to visit her. Their affection for her is readily apparent. She has commented, in fact, that one of her challenges is to provide a caring environment without encouraging students to act out just so they can

PUT TOGETHER A "PROGRAM" OF PROGRAMS. When we attend a play or concert, we often receive a "program" that gives the essential details about the production. Parents, new students, (and many teachers) would appreciate a brief "Program of Programs" that gives the essential details about services the school provides; the name of the program (including what the letters mean for acronyms); the name, telephone number, and E-mail address of the person responsible; and a short summary of the services available. Students themselves could create these programs as a way to display their talents. ♪

come visit!

This program, and others like it, demonstrate a powerful blending of structure and support. Students who make "bad" choices are treated with respect and optimism. They are trusted, in an intentional fashion, to learn to make better decisions. Most of all, they receive the caring attention of a teacher who is their advocate as well as their supervisor. Safe schools are places where people are treated decently.

Processes

The fifth and final "P," processes, is embedded in the people, places, policies, and programs of the school. Simply stated, processes "are the way we do things around here." While often implanted in the culture itself, processes are so important that they deserve special attention in this concluding section.

It seems self-evident that students who are consistently treated with respect are far less likely to cause problems in the classroom. Conversely, students who think the system is out to embarrass them and who believe the teacher treats them as though they are worthless, unable, and irresponsible, will find ways to disrupt or destroy the places, policies, programs, and people involved. This has been true throughout history whenever humans have experienced discontent and resentment.

Perhaps nowhere is this tendency to revolt against circumstances portrayed more powerfully than in the words of Shakespeare's hunchback Richard, who angrily proclaimed: "And therefore, since I cannot prove a lover to entertain these fair well-spoken days, I am determined to prove a villain, and hate the idle pleasures of these days" (*Richard III,* Act I, Scene I). The rule is clear: People do unto others as they have been done unto. Because this is so, it is critical that each process found in the school should telegraph messages to each person who enters a school each day that he or she is able, valuable, and responsible and should behave accordingly.

PROMOTE PARTICIPATION. Encourage students to participate in decision-making processes. Students who are unable to make any decisions that concern them soon become passive and lethargic. In time, they are likely to revolt against the people, policies, programs, and processes that deny them the opportunity to help make decisions that influence their lives. ♪

The process of assigning penalties and punishments is particularly sensitive. Penalties should not have destructive effects. For example, the processes should not teach that power is absolute, that penalties and punishments are disproportionately applied to minority group members, or that they are applied with little or no regard to due process. Most students have a keen sense of justice. Unfair or unjust processes can create immediate trouble as well as long-lasting resentment. An inappropriate or uncaring process can be very disinviting.

Perhaps the most valuable processes for promoting self-discipline are those at work during private conferences with students. The teacher who talks with a student during a planning period, or before or after school, gives both parties an opportunity to understand one another better and to explore opportunities for resolving problems and realizing potential. Such private talks provide both the teacher and student an opportunity to talk "off stage," away from the attention of other students that can escalate difficulties. In such conferences, students often provide the solutions to their own discipline problems and other concerns as well. In conferences with middle and junior high students over the years, the authors have identified learning difficulties, resolved inter-student conflicts, detected learning disabilities, discovered problems of alcohol and drug abuse, and opened doors to counseling, remediation, and continued development. None of these outcomes would have been possible without private conferences.

A powerful procedure for connecting and highlighting the five P's is the G.O.A.L.S. process developed by the International Alliance for Invitational Education (Purkey & Strahan, 1995). G.O.A.L.S. provides a strategy for involving all teachers and staff in assessing and planning school improvements. The five basic steps are Goal setting, Outlining actions, Anticipating obstacles, Listing alternatives, and Specifying action plans.

The G.O.A.L.S. process begins by organizing participants into five "strand teams," one team for each of the Five Powerful P's (People, Places, Policies, Programs, and Processes). These teams meet in a faculty meeting, teacher work day, or after school to think about ways to make the school more inviting from their own assigned strand. Ideally, each team includes an administrator, several teachers, staff members, parents, and students. One representative from each strand team serves on a "steering committee" that coordinates the G.O.A.L.S. process. The basic procedure is as follows:

- Goal setting – Each team brainstorms possibilities for inviting school success using its own particular "P." The team then lists a set of 3-5 priority goals for creating this success.
- Outlining actions – Each team "passes" its list of goals to a second team. Members of this second team review the goals listed by the first team and outlines *actions* to accomplish these goals.
- Anticipating obstacles – Each team passes the list of goals and actions to a third team who anticipates obstacles, listing possible barriers and stating all the "yes, but..." concerns that may limit action.
- Listing alternatives – Each team now passes the list of goals, actions, and obstacles to a fourth team who identifies alternative solutions that may address the obstacles identified.
- Specifying action plans – The entire set of notes is now returned to the original strand team who uses this feedback to develop a specific action plan.

This process features structure and collaboration. We have used this procedure with a number of groups and observed that it promotes involvement and helps generate consensus.

The original goals return to each team enriched with new ideas and suggestions from all the other teams. Accordingly, the action plans that emerge are more sophisticated than those developed initially. Almost everyone has seen the goals, has offered advice, identified obstacles, and suggested ways to overcome obstacles. When the strand teams present their final plans to their colleagues, everyone has a sense of ownership. This process yields creative and useful ideas for reform, and, at the same time, encourages a sense that school reform is an ongoing process rather than a fixed agenda. By involving everyone in addressing all of the five P's, this process approaches reform in a comprehensive manner and helps participants see how everything is connected in the "whole bowl of Jell-O" that is the school culture.

Summary

The dynamics of Invitational Teaching grow richer and stronger when supported by a school culture that nurtures success and self-discipline. Studies of school reform have shown that the most powerful school cultures promote "significance" by pursuing moral purpose – to make a difference in the lives of students, families, and communities.

The five Powerful P's of Invitational Education provide a framework for improving school culture. Growth begins with *people* who are committed to the stance of Invitational Teaching, becomes more concrete and specific as *places* grow more inviting, and takes shape with *policies* that state expectations and avoid discrimination. Over time, *programs* offer structure and support to students, teachers and parents. *Processes* promote collaboration and provide recurring procedures for assessing and guiding growth. As a result, the whole bowl of Jell-O that is school culture grows richer and stronger, providing a supportive environment for the dynamics of good discipline that enhance the quality of life in classrooms. ♫

4.

THE INVITATIONAL FRAMEWORK IN ACTION

Studies of successful middle school teachers depict them as exciting, enthusiastic, energizing people, ones who relish the day-to-day life of classrooms and who enjoy the company of young people. Bottom line: *the teacher's self is the most important factor in any classroom.*

This chapter focuses on four basic areas of the teacher's life in which Invitational Teaching can be applied: (1) being personally inviting with oneself, (2) being personally inviting with others, (3) being professionally inviting with oneself, and (4) being professionally inviting with others. While the following concepts are simple, they are not easy. The Invitational Teacher is one who can balance the demands of the four areas and orchestrate the ways they blend together to produce a productive and humane classroom environment.

Being Personally Inviting with Oneself

While many aspects of education are complicated, one basic principle remains clear: *to maintain a healthy classroom it is essential for the teacher to invite himself or herself personally.* This invitation is to maintain one's own personal energy level and to nurture oneself psychologically, physically, and intellectually.

Psychologically

Experienced teachers understand the need to have control over their expressed emotions, particularly when working with students who offer difficult challenges. The teacher's ability to control one's own emotions in the face of extreme adversity increases the likelihood that he or she will be able to understand and influence the course of student behavior.

There are many ways of being personally inviting with oneself psychologically. Learning meditation and relaxation techniques, talking with a good friend and colleague, keeping a diary, communing with nature, are samples of the countless opportunities available to teachers. Because few professions are so demanding psychologically as teaching, it is vital that teachers work on their own psychological well-being.

BUILD A PERSONAL FORT KNOX. Start a special file of letters, awards, notes, cards, and other recognitions you have received over the years. When you begin to feel down or "burned out," visit your own Fort Knox and restore your spirits. ♪

One practical way to invite oneself psychologically is to practice positive "self talk," to monitor what one says to oneself internally and to "clean up" false, demeaning, or negative narrations. Reminding oneself of one's own positive abilities has tremendous advantages. When a recent "teacher of the year" was asked how she maintains her enthusiasm for teaching, she responded that she had the following statement taped on the dashboard of her car, and she reads it to herself on the way to school: "I know what I'm doing. I know my students. I know we're going to enjoy learning today!"

The process of modifying cognitive processes by monitoring and changing "self-talk" was introduced by Meichenbaum (1977) and expanded by Purkey (2000). As explained by Purkey, the goal is to learn different ways of looking at reality by altering what we say *about* ourselves *to* ourselves internally – on a semi-conscious level. Cognitions influence behavior, and when teachers alter their cognitions, they alter their behavior. For instance, rather than thinking "I can't," use "I won't," "I don't," or "I would find it difficult." By changing such cognitive processes as "always" to "often," "never" to "rarely," and "I must" to "I want," teachers can inoculate themselves against many environmental stressors (Meichenbaum, 1977; Purkey, 2000).

One important part of being personally inviting with oneself psychologically is allowing oneself avenues of emotional release. This may mean crying at a sad movie, laughing until your sides hurt over a joke, cheering at a baseball game, or engaging in happy, child-like play at a party. Beyond these more public demonstrations, a private chuckle at one's own mistakes, feeling a sense of anger over an injustice, or imagining delightful fantasies are all part of being personally inviting with oneself psychologically. A valuable resource is *Living Intentionally and Making Life Happen* (Schmidt, 1994).

Intellectually

A second component of being personally inviting with oneself is to stay alive intellectually. To avoid boredom it is necessary to participate in numerous activities that increase the information base, sharpen thought pro-

FIGHT BOREDOM. If you become bored with teaching, it is likely that you have become boring. A "cardinal sin" of teaching is to bore students to death. When you find ways to make the classroom exciting, you make your lessons more interesting for yourself as well as for your students. ♪

cesses, strengthen the ability to generalize conditions, and improve the overall powers of the mind.

Studies of adult learners returning to school have shown that new learning opportunities can revitalize "body and soul" as well as mind. Benefits of new learning far exceed "retooling" for jobs. One of the key incentives for returning to school is *pleasure* – the joy of new ideas, re-awakened brainpower, and increased self-esteem.

Teachers can enjoy similar "renewal" benefits with or without taking new courses. Among the many ways to stay alive intellectually is to read extensively on a variety of subjects, to visit museums, cultural centers, zoos, parks, galleries, and exhibits. It also is advantageous to join and participate in organizations such as historical societies, political groups, garden clubs, and other special interest groups. (Long lists of civic, cultural, scientific, political, and hobby groups are available from most Chambers of Commerce.) If the teacher is located away from a city, there are still local organizations involved in exciting ventures. The main thing is to get in the game! Teachers who are well read and intellectually alive are more likely to have students who are interested in course content and well behaved in the classroom.

KEEP UP TO DATE. When it is clear to students that the teacher knows what he or she is talking about, and can relate this knowledge to the personal worlds of students, misbehavior is less frequent and more easily controlled. The relation between the teacher and his or her subject matter is critical to good teaching. ♪

Physically

Teaching is a profession that is as demanding physically as it is intellectually and psychologically. It is vital that teachers who wish to maintain good classroom discipline strive for good physical health. This means intentionally restricting high cholesterol foods and slowing down on the use of sugar, salt, alcohol, and other ingredients that may threaten wellness. A commitment to wellness extends to exercising regularly, eliminating smoking or other habits that contribute to sickness, and drinking water in preference to other kinds of liquids. The many ways to be personally inviting with oneself are so numerous that the ones mentioned here are only illustrative. But together they suggest a wellness lifestyle: to eat properly, exercise regularly, dress comfortably, drink reasonably, stand tall, and get sufficient rest.

> *GET IN THE GAME. Life is not a spectator sport, so find a way to exercise. Successful teachers know that they can be more effective in the classroom when they work to maintain their own physical health. Whether it is an organized sport or an individual activity, it is vital to find a way to exercise.* ♪

Being Personally Inviting with Others

Someone once said about students: "They may not remember what you taught them, but they always remember how you treated them." This comment exemplifies the importance of being personally inviting with other human beings. Through sharing the company of significant others, and through countless inviting acts given and received, the principles of trust, intentionality, respect, and optimism are nourished and enriched.

Nurturing friendships

After making a presentation to a graduate class, a veteran middle grades teacher was asked, "You seem so excited about middle school, what is it that you like so much about this age group?" The teacher replied that he had not always been so enthusiastic and told the story of his first years in teaching. He began teaching only because he wanted to coach and was very disappointed to get his first job in a middle school. He longed to be reassigned to the high school "where the real teams played."

CHECK THE CALENDAR. Are there people in your professional world whom you admire and would like to know better? If so, be brave! Invite them to lunch. If you invite, they may accept, but if you don't, they can't. ♪

During the first fateful year, several friends changed his life. One was a fellow teacher who came to him repeatedly with offers to help and encouragement to try new ideas in his classes. Another was the principal who asked him to teach in that building a second year. "He saw something in me that I wasn't seeing," the teacher suggested. The people who made the biggest difference were the students themselves. "I found myself getting caught up in their boundless energy and enthusiasm," he noted. The following year, when he was asked to become an assistant high school football coach and move to that building, he declined the offer and has remained a middle school teacher ever since.

Friends are the teacher's best life support system. A close friend of the authors once commented that all the professional success in the world will not make up for loss of success with the people you love and who love you. It is difficult to over-estimate the value of friendships. Invitations sent between friends equal the power of invitations sent to oneself because they affirm both individuals in the relationship. It is through friendships that teachers celebrate their kinship with colleagues, students, and all humanity.

One additional note regarding friendships is that they are like a garden – they require attention and nourishment. With cultivation they are likely to develop and deepen. Without attention, they tend to wither and die.

McGinnis (1979) offered five ways to deepen friendships: (1) Assign priority to your friendships, (2) allow others to know you as a person, (3) talk openly about your affection, (4) learn the gestures of affection (such as gift-giving and rituals), and (5) create space in your relationships so that your friends have room to expand and develop. These and other ways to cultivate friendships can be learned, but they must be learned again and again – there is no end to the adventure of nourishing friendships.

Celebrating life

A further way of being personally inviting with others is to celebrate life. This celebration is much more than fireworks, parades, and party time. It exists at a deeper level where the significance and richness of life are more fully appreciated.

CELEBRATE SPECIAL OCCASIONS. Birthdays and other special events (a new baby, holidays, an engagement, etc.) are meant to be a time for hoopla. A private calendar on his or her desk will help the teacher to remember occasions. Even the grouchiest student or colleague may light up at a special little event in his or her honor. ♪

Celebration reflects the concepts of trust in oneself and optimism for life. More specifically, the celebration of life involves a particular attitude toward living that the teacher takes and maintains. The unexpected bonus from all this is that those who are intentionally inviting with themselves and others are more likely to develop friendships and celebrate life.

Being Professionally Inviting with Oneself

New and exciting things are always happening in education. Innovative approaches to the teaching/learning process are everywhere. Trying to keep up is like trying to get a drink of water from a fire hose! Yet teachers are responsible for being informed about ideas and trends that have an impact on their performance. This responsibility can best be met by the teacher's practice of being professionally inviting with oneself: to accept the challenge of being a lifelong learner, to try new ways of teaching, and to stay fresh professionally.

Becoming a lifelong learner

Successful teachers quickly discover that their educational skills, methods, and knowledge must be constantly upgraded. They recognize the importance of learning new techniques, understanding emerging research findings, improving their professional functioning, and rekindling their enthusiasm for teaching.

Becoming and being a lifelong learner means reading up-to-date books, enrolling in refresher courses at colleges and universities, working towards an advanced degree, attending professional conferences and summer workshops, entering the world of computers, and even, if available, taking a semester or a year of sabbatical leave to refresh oneself personally and professionally.

A growing problem in education is the concept of teacher "burnout." To avoid stagnant in-a-rut teaching it is necessary to get in the game of life by becoming a lifelong learner. One way to get in the game is to conduct one's own research, either quantitative or qualitative, then having the courage to present one's ideas and findings at local, state, provincial, regional, national, or international professional meetings. Presenting a program or workshop is a great way of being professionally inviting with oneself while also sharing one's work with other educators.

HONOR THE RULE OF FOUR. When a teacher spends time doing classroom chores that a volunteer could do just as well with four hours or less of training, the "rule of four" may be applied. Train parents or other adult volunteers to do as many of the routine activities as possible (filing papers, completing forms, duplicating materials, one-to-one tutoring, etc.) so that the teacher can concentrate on instruction. ♪

Another strategy for avoiding burnout is to imagine how life would be different if one did, in fact, leave teaching. Many "new teachers" are former teachers returning. When interviewed, returning teachers consistently describe how higher salaries in other jobs did not make up for the "lost joys" of teaching. One said he would often look at the clock and think of what he would be doing at school at that hour.

Exploring new frontiers

Taking a few risks and exploring new possibilities is central to the stance of Invitational Teaching. This exploration might include swapping classes with a teacher from another school or school system, running for office in one of the many educational organizations, or applying for funds to conduct some creative programs or action research. Professional development means keeping one's blade bright – not rusting on one's laurels. The teacher who follows the Invitational Education model works to progress through successfully higher levels of personal and professional functioning. This requires a lifelong commitment to be professionally inviting with oneself. This leads directly to the process of being professionally inviting with others.

Being Professionally Inviting With Others

The major focus of this book is on ways to be professionally inviting with others – to create and maintain a productive, humane, and well-managed classroom environment. Yet it is important in this chapter to reemphasize several aspects of being professionally inviting with others, including communicating clearly and evaluating fairly.

Communicating clearly

The responsibility for any communication lies with the sender. The teacher should present guidelines for acceptable classroom behavior in a clear and firm manner. *There should be no doubt in students' minds what is acceptable and unacceptable behavior.*

Upon presenting clear guidelines, the teacher follows up by giving reasons for the conduct code and invites students' reactions and suggestions. If the teacher experiences difficulty in giving logical reasons for each rule, it is likely that the rule is unclear, unreasonable, and ultimately unenforceable – and

BE A CLOCK-WATCHER. A classroom clock in easy view of everyone will help the teacher start and end classes on time. Promptness on the teacher's part establishes an "on time" – "on task" – "well organized" classroom climate.♪

the students will readily note this.

Communicating clearly also involves emphasizing positive behavior. For example, "We have ten minutes left and it is important that we finish on time" is clear and more positive than "You students will have to stay in after school if you are not finished on time." The point is to communicate clear expectations: that these expectations are reasonable, that "we are intelligent people, and that we are working together to create and maintain a productive classroom."

Treating students fairly

It is difficult to overestimate how important it is that the teacher treat all students fairly. Unfortunately, there is evidence that there are many students in North American schools who see themselves as being treated unfairly, that "No one in this school cares whether I live or die." Their unhappy perceptions are supported by research that indicates that minority students and slow learners are treated less equitably than others (Simpson & Erickson, 1983; Gouldner, 1978). Good and Brophy (1980, 1984) presented evidence that students labeled as slow learners are seated farther from the teacher's desk, are given less time to respond to teachers' questions, and are generally isolated. Such unfair treatment appears to have a subtle but profound negative impact on academic achievement, self-concept as learner, and classroom behavior.

KNOW WHEN TO ASK FOR BACK-UP. Classroom discipline is primarily the responsibility of the classroom teacher. The teacher should seek outside assistance (sending students to the office, calling security) only when it is really needed. Sending students out often undermines the teacher's authority. At the same time, waiting too long may let a situation get out of hand. This balancing act is part of the art of good teaching. ♪

Being professionally inviting with students requires the teacher to intentionally guard against differential treatment. This means systematically organizing the classroom so that each student is invited each day in some way. Ways to accomplish this goal include rotating assignments, re-arranging seating, and using cards to call on students systematically rather than relying on hand-raising or random selection.

Finally, treating students fairly involves the clear recognition that students in a democratic society have protections under the law. In the landmark case *Tinker v. Des Moines Independent Community School District* (1969), the Honorable Abe Fortas, Associate Justice of Supreme Court of the United States, wrote: "School officials do not possess absolute authority over students. Students in school as well as out of school are "persons" under our Constitution. They are possessed of fundamental rights which the state must respect" (US 503 & 511, 393). When carrying out any policy, program, or process designed to create and maintain good classroom discipline, it is important that it be perceived by the people involved as inherently fair and appropriately administered.

Summary

This chapter has presented the four areas embedded in Invitational Teaching that are important to successful personal and professional functioning. These are (1) being personally inviting with oneself, (2) being personally inviting with others, (3) being professionally inviting with oneself, and (4) being professionally inviting with others. Successful teachers are able to orchestrate these four areas into a seamless whole of personal and professional living.

Being personally inviting with oneself is the first step in becoming an Invitational Teacher. Teachers who take care of themselves emotionally, intellectually, and physically are in the best position to be a beneficial presence in the lives of students. Being personally inviting with others provides the teacher with the necessary "life support" system of people who care for the teacher and for whom the teacher cares deeply. Being professionally inviting with oneself incorporates a willingness to explore, take risks, and "get in the game." Continuous lifelong learning reflects such willingness. Finally, being professionally inviting with others is the heart of education and the key to positive classroom discipline. ♫

5.

CLASSROOM PRACTICES THAT PROMOTE SELF-DISCIPLINE

Successful teachers are well aware that there are no sure-fire "cookbooks" for maintaining good classroom discipline. It would be wonderful to be able to reach for *Ms. Smith's Favorite Recipes For Good Behavior,* but great teachers, like great chefs, understand that success is far more than following a recipe. Success comes from a consistent philosophy of teaching, coupled with an understanding of underlying processes, a repertoire of practical techniques, and careful timing.

Although there are no cookbook solutions for good discipline, studies of successful teachers have documented three powerful features that characterize their classrooms:

1. Successful classroom management promotes self-discipline.
2. Successful classroom management begins with Academic Learning Time.
3. Successful classroom management promotes academic achievement.

In the section that follows, we present summaries of research reports that have demonstrated the power of these three key features. To illustrate the impact of these features we offer examples of classroom practices that promote good discipline (blue) or elicit bad behavior (orange).

Promoting Self-Discipline

As we have emphasized repeatedly, Invitational Teaching asserts that all students are valuable, able, and responsible and are capable of behaving accordingly. Invitational Teachers find ways to link these three beliefs in guiding students to improve self-discipline. Their students see themselves as more valuable when they know that their teacher cares about them as individuals and expects them to behave themselves. They grow more able as they make better decisions. They learn to be more responsible when their teachers affirm their responsibilities and hold them accountable for their behavior.

Glasser's work with troubled adolescents demonstrated the power of self-discipline (Glasser, 1965, 1974, 1986, 1993). When provided with supportive professional counselors and caring classroom teachers, students who had previously demonstrated low self-esteem and antisocial behavior learned to accept responsibility for their actions and make healthier decisions. Glasser found that students who misbehave are almost always trying to establish "control" in inappropriate ways: avoiding schoolwork, seeking attention, creating diversions, or playing power games. His "control theory" framework (1986) emphasized the need to help students

DEVELOP CLASS RULES TOGETHER. When teachers involve students in developing classroom rules and procedures, they feel a stronger sense of ownership in the classroom. In our experience, students take this responsibility seriously. Through careful discussion and deliberation, they almost always generate clear, workable rules and procedures. Then, if a rule is broken, they experience a stronger commitment to "shared responsibility," even when they are the ones who break the rule. ♪

understand that they choose their behaviors and to guide them in accepting responsibility for their choices. Glasser's studies showed that students gain self-discipline when they believe they can trust caring adults, are treated as responsible, and when they experience success (p. 39).

Jones' (1996) review of research on classroom management underscores the importance of a caring environment in helping students learn self-discipline. As Jones found, "At its best, classroom management is not only a means to effective instruction, it also becomes a vehicle for providing students with a sense of community and with increased skills in interpersonal communication, conflict management, and self-control" (p. 503).

Attaining Academic Learning Time

For more than twenty years, researchers have consistently documented the importance of learning time in the classroom. In their review of studies of "factors that influence achievement," Good and Brophy (2000) emphasized the impact of student engagement, noting that achievement is strongly associated with active learning (p. 29). Fisher and his colleagues (1978) shaped much of our understanding of these relationships in their now classic studies that focused on the role of teachers in fostering student achievement. They identified the power of "Academic Learning Time," that is, the actual time students spend engaged in classroom tasks they view as purposeful. In study after study, students in the classrooms of teachers who consistently promoted Academic Learning Time (ALT) outperformed their counterparts in classrooms with significantly less ALT. A growing number of investigations have confirmed these findings (Jones, 1996).

CONSULT WITH STUDENTS WHEN PLANNING PROJECT OPTIONS. Students appreciate having a voice in developing learning activities. Choices make them feel more valuable, able, and responsible and increase Academic Learning Time. Teachers can increase the power of the choices they offer by asking students to suggest ways to present their ideas. Their suggestions have included making videos, creating "musical collages" by assembling selected parts of songs, creating web sites, and making board games to report their insights. ♪

In one of the most comprehensive investigations, Wang, Haertel, and Walberg (1993) integrated results from more than 179 studies that examined 228 variables related to student achievement. Results showed that the most important factor in promoting student learning was "maintaining active participation by all students" (p. 257). In a series of meta-analyses, Hattie (1992, 1996) analyzed over 200,000 studies and generated a statistical model based on effect size of variables. The essential attributes of teacher expertise were providing feedback to enhance student learning, involving students in challenging tasks, structuring classroom activities to promote engagement, and classroom management that engages and teaches all students (Hattie, Jaeger, Strahan, & Baker, 1998). Clark and associates (1995) found that students with a history of behavior problems learned to behave themselves better when they were systematically involved in selecting learning tasks that matched their interests. These extensive studies document what successful teachers have long understood: *active engagement is the fundamental condition of student achievement.*

Practices That Invite Self-Discipline and Academic Learning Time

As researchers have learned more about the ways that successful teachers promote self-discipline and attain Academic Learning Time, they have identified specific classroom management practices that accomplish these interrelated goals. More than thirty years ago, Kounin (1970) found four recurring techniques that successful teachers used to promote engagement and minimize disruptions. Since that time, these four techniques have become the hallmark of preventive discipline:

- Withitness – monitoring classroom activities with heightened awareness. Students sometimes refer to this as "the teacher who has eyes in the back of her head."
- Overlapping – carrying out several essential tasks simultaneously. Students often note that "the teacher can do two or three things at once."
- Signal continuity and momentum – maintaining the flow of lessons. Students appreciate teachers who can "let us know when to listen and pay attention" and "keep things going."
- Variety and challenge – adjusting lessons in response to students' needs. Students value teachers who "break it up and keep things interesting."

Good and Brophy (2000) emphasized that research has continued to demonstrate the effectiveness of these techniques. As they explained,

> The key to successful classroom management is a proactive approach that features

> clarity in communicating expectations. Three characteristics of this proactive approach are: (1) it is preventive rather that just reactive; (2) it integrates management methods that encourage student conduct with instructional methods that encourage student achievement of curricular objectives; and (3) it focuses on managing the class as a group, not just on the behavior of individual students (p. 126).

These proactive practices fit well with the Jell-O principle presented in Chapter Three and provide a strong foundation for good discipline. Even so, we have found that the ways in which they are combined determine success. The difference between ordinary teachers and Invitational Teachers lies in the ways they combine principles and skills into a seamless pattern of personal and professional functioning. The "good discipline sequence" that we have identified in our work with Invitational Teachers helps describe some of this artistry.

The Good Discipline Sequence

Several models have presented stages or steps in establishing good discipline (Glasser, 1974; Curwin & Mendler, 1988; Charles, 1992). The specific sequence presented here is based on one created originally by Purkey and Novak (1984) and extended by Purkey and Schmidt (1987, 1996). It contains a preparation stage, an initiating/responding stage, and a follow-up stage. Each of these stages contains four steps. The stages and steps are depicted in Figure One.

Figure 1
The Good Discipline Sequence

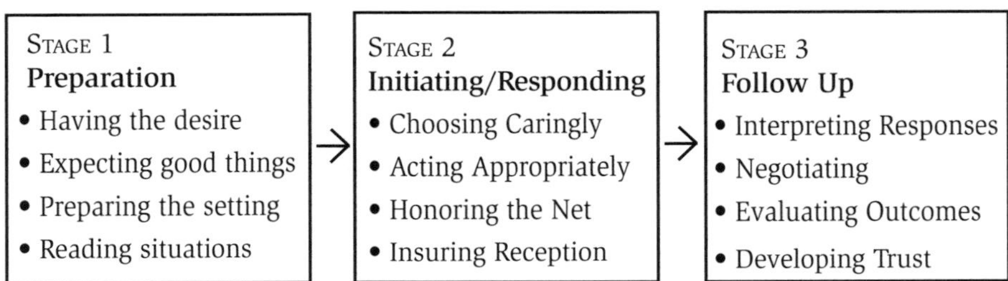

Preparation stage

The preparation stage of Invitational Teaching consists of four steps: having the desire, expecting good things, preparing the setting, and reading the situation. It will be useful to see how each of these steps relates to good discipline.

Having the desire. It may seem obvious, but wanting to create and maintain good classroom discipline is an essential first step. As Glenda, The Good Witch of the North, reminded Dorothy in the 1939 MGM film classic *The Wizard of Oz:* "Dear Dorothy, you've always had the power, you just didn't want hard enough." Without the intentional desire to create and maintain good classroom discipline, all of the following stages and steps are useless.

This desire is more than a feeling or a wish. It is a commitment to developing *shared control* in the classroom. In the first chapter, we emphasized that becoming an Invitational Teacher requires a definite point of view. In contrast to views of education that view teaching as something that the teacher does to students or as command-and-control, Invitational Teachers seek to promote self-control through collaboration. This belief, that students are valuable, able, and responsible, is the foundation of the Invitational Stance.

In their analysis of reasons why some teachers adopt a "get tough stance" in their classrooms, Reed and Strahan (1995) found that "how we view the concept of control" shapes the ways we respond to discipline problems (p. 327). Some teachers manifest a "control orientation" that believes that "if students are given the opportunity, they will become disruptive and that teachers must maintain a no-nonsense posture" (p. 327). In some schools, this belief is so pervasive that it has become a shared value among many of the teachers. "Having the desire" requires teachers to examine their beliefs toward control. If a teacher finds that he or she has a tendency to manifest a control orientation, it will be necessary to question that belief and to find ways to develop more positive expectations toward students.

> *CHECK THE ABSENCE LIST AS A CHECK ON YOUR ATTITUDE. Most teachers check the absence list each morning to see if any of their students will miss class. The way they check the list provides clues to the way that they perceive individual students. If the teacher feels a tendency to rejoice when finding a certain student's name on the absence list, that is a good sign that the teacher needs to reflect on his or her attitude and that the student needs a special invitation to feel valuable, able, and responsible.* ♪

Expecting good things. In their review of the literature on teacher expectations, Good and Brophy (2000) concluded

> The implications of all of this seems to be that teachers should form and project expectations that are as positive as they can be while still remaining realistic. Such expecta-

> tions should represent genuine beliefs about what can be achieved and therefore should be taken seriously as goals toward which to work in instructing students. (p. 107)

By expecting good things of oneself and of students, the teacher is in an excellent position to invite positive classroom discipline.

An experience of one of the authors with a middle student demonstrates how important "having the desire" and "expecting good things" can be. Steve entered my middle school classroom with a reputation as a "bully" and "troublemaker." His elementary teachers had documented a wide range of disruptive behaviors and academic needs. They recommended that he be placed in the remedial reading program. When Steve first arrived, he shoved his way into the reading room and announced loudly that he did not need any "dummy class" and did not plan to stay. Through caring and appropriate behavior over a period of several weeks I was able to assure Steve that he need not feel threatened by the reading program. Still, Steve demonstrated little enthusiasm for his work or respect for other people.

> It was only when I began to teach the basic rules of chess as a means of encouraging logical thinking that Steve began to get involved in the class. I encouraged Steve to join the school chess team and, when he began to attend, asked him to participate in an upcoming tournament. When Steve decided he did not want to compete, I asked

> Steve to supervise the refreshment stand and keep track of the money. This experience proved to be a turning point for Steve. His responsibility for scheduling other students for the refreshment stand and keeping the money box were very visible reminders that he was able, valuable, and responsible. While Steve did not become a chess "champion," a "great" reader, or a model student, he did make real progress with both his reading and his behavior after becoming refreshment stand manager.

This vignette demonstrates that good discipline begins with intentional desire and positive expectations. It also underscores the importance of taking a "long range" view of the situation. Steve needed time to develop new ways of responding to situations and to other people.

Preparing the setting. Having the desire and expecting good things are necessary for good discipline, but they are not sufficient in themselves. A third important step in classroom management is preparing the setting in which positive discipline takes place. Invitational Teachers manage the physical environment as much as possible. This means keeping a close eye on such supportive or distracting factors as lighting, temperature, furniture (size, arrangement and proximity), barriers to student visibility, nature of decorations, the quality of equipment, colors, signs, and even sound levels. The orange and blue metaphor is a good reminder that *everything in and around the classroom adds to or subtracts from successful classroom management*.

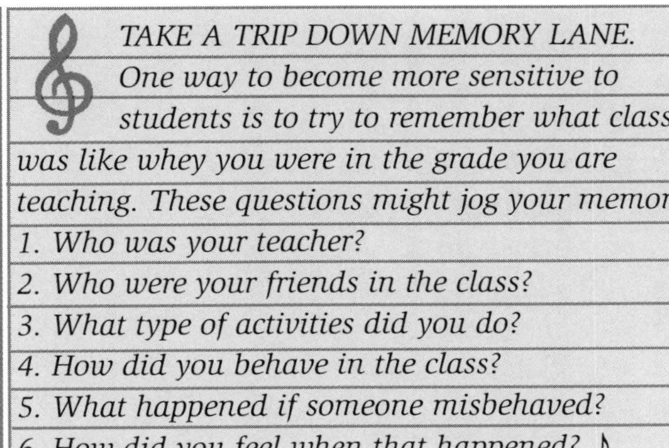

TAKE A TRIP DOWN MEMORY LANE. One way to become more sensitive to students is to try to remember what class was like whey you were in the grade you are teaching. These questions might jog your memory:

1. Who was your teacher?
2. Who were your friends in the class?
3. What type of activities did you do?
4. How did you behave in the class?
5. What happened if someone misbehaved?
6. How did you feel when that happened? ♪

An excellent example of how setting can be supportive of good discipline may be found at Guilford Middle School (in Guilford County, North Carolina). Students are encouraged to feel able, valuable, and responsible from the moment that they enter the school grounds. Creating a caring and appropriate environment is a continuing effort of faculty, staff, and students. While the building itself is old, the physical setting is attractive. Plants adorn entrances to the building. Student work is displayed everywhere. Classrooms are kaleidoscopes of projects and displays. Although teachers, secretaries, and principals are very "busy" with the tasks of the day, no one is ever too busy to recognize a visitor, talk with a student, answer questions, send a friendly greeting, or practice common courtesy. Moreover, the school demonstrates positive "effective outcomes." Achievement scores surpass state standards; attendance is high, and vandalism and violence rare. As students and staff will attest, success has not just happened. It is the result of a wide range of intentional efforts to make the school setting as exciting, caring, and supportive as possible.

Reading situations. Being sensitive to what is taking place in the classroom has been called "empathy," "interpersonal

DEVELOP LINEBACKER'S EYES. In football, linebackers are expected to watch everything that happens on the field. Successful teachers are able to meet the needs of individual students while continuing a group activity. This means answering the questions of one student while continuing the group lesson. The secret is maintaining good eye contact with both the individual student and the group. ♪

perceptivity," "social intelligence," and "withitness." All of these attributes involve the ability to read situations. At heart, reading situations means the ability to understand and predict what others are feeling and what they are likely to do at a particular time and place. This ability to understand and interpret the signal systems of the classroom is one of the characteristics of expert teachers (Smith, 1999). They do not get distracted from the responsibility of maintaining good discipline. Understanding students' feelings and likely behaviors is essential in maintaining good discipline because it forms a bridge between the teacher's behaviors and those of students.

One additional element in reading situations is understanding the nature of middle grade students. Students undergo a dramatic series of developmental changes during their middle school years that bewilder them as well as their parents and teachers (Van Hoose, Strahan, & L'Esperance, 2001). The physical changes that accompany the onset of puberty are perhaps the most dramatic of any time in life. Psychological and intellectual changes are equally profound. These changes in how students think are intertwined with new perceptions of self and others. The many changes create a backdrop of "unpredictability" for everything that occurs in and around the middle school.

Middle level students sometimes find it difficult to concentrate on their schoolwork. Some portion of this difficulty is the result of the physical changes they are experiencing. During "growth spurts" in height and weight, students experience hormonal fluctuation. This results in varying energy levels. One minute the students will be "bouncing" off walls, desks, chairs, and each other, only to "fade off" the next. Bone and muscle tissue grow at different rates, making it painfully difficult to sit still for long periods of time, especially on hard chairs. Understanding these changes, adjusting to them, and planning strategies for nurturing positive discipline are critical dimensions in reading situations.

HANG A MIRROR. Obtain a full-length mirror and place it somewhere in the classroom where students can see themselves as they pass by. This invites neatness, good grooming, and a sense of pride. These are basic to self-discipline. Hanging a mirror also shows students that the teacher understands how important students consider their appearance. ♪

At some point during the adolescent period most students find it necessary to "test limits" and establish independence from family. These efforts are based on the emerging need to understand "Who am I?" During this period of rapid changes in body and mind, students are hungry to feel good about themselves. Self-concepts are being negotiated in new ways, and students are struggling to become what they desire to be. It is this subjective self perception, reflected in what students say to themselves, that plays a dominant influence on students' success or failure in school (Purkey, 2000).

The school is a critical setting in the development of student self-concept as learner. It provides students with countless opportunities to interact with an array of people and to discuss topics different from those considered earlier in life. School also offers the opportunity to try new behaviors. It is important to remember that good students on occasion will do bad things. How a teacher handles disciplinary situations may be a critical factor in determining whether the teacher is a beneficial presence, or a lethal one, in each student's efforts to develop a positive and realistic self-image.

Initiating/responding stage

As indicated in Figure One, the Initial Preparation Stage cultivates the ground for the second stage of the good discipline sequence, the Initiating/Responding Stage. It is this critical stage that provides opportunities for students to accept and maintain responsibility for their classroom behavior. The Initiating/Responding Stage also contains four steps:

(1) choosing caringly
(2) acting appropriately
(3) honoring the net
(4) ensuring reception.

Choosing caringly. In making the right moves in the classroom, teachers benefit by having the most up-to-date information about their students. Current knowledge about the student (including what is happening in his or her world) gives the teacher the ability to choose the most caring and appropriate “blue” summons to good behavior that are most

> *REMIND STUDENTS TO BELIEVE IN THEMSELVES. When students make mistakes or demonstrate poor judgment, this creates a "teachable moment" for the teacher. It is a great time to talk with the student and offer encouragement. When teachers let students know that they believe students can work things out, solve problems, and improve performance, they promote responsibility and trust.* ♪

likely to be accepted and acted upon successfully.

In choosing caringly, Purkey and Schmidt (1987) point out that teacher invitations are most likely to be accepted and acted upon successfully by students when seven conditions are present: (1) the invitation appears safe to accept, (2) there are repeated opportunities to accept the invitation, (3) good things have happened when invitations have been accepted in the past, (4) it is in keeping with norms governing social behavior, (5) the invitation is clear and unambiguous, (6) the student believes that he or she is able and willing to live up to the expectations involved in the invitation, and (7) the invitation is not too demanding in intensity or duration. *The classroom teacher directly influences all seven of these factors.* Thus, initial invitations should be simple, short-term, not too demanding, and above all, caring and appropriate in their sensitivity to student feelings.

Acting appropriately. While choosing caringly is the first step in the Initiating/responding stage, an equally important step is acting appropriately. There are countless less-than-successful teachers who consistently make their choices based on a great deal of care but who seem to be out of focus when it comes to acting appropriately. For example, awarding a banner for "best-behaved" class may be a big hit with first graders, but middle school students would be mortified! Choosing caringly is vital, but the choice must be accompanied by appropriate action.

Inviting good discipline in the middle school requires a student/teacher relationship that consistently strives to remedy current concerns while increasing the likelihood of future good behavior. This relationship is most likely to develop when the teacher makes realistic plans of action and acts upon them in a caring and appropriate manner.

Acting appropriately is a matter of deciding how best to invite students to participate in the task at hand. A useful strategy is to handle situations at the lowest possible level using the least amount of time and energy. For example, in a situation where students begin a private conversation in the middle of a lesson, a raised eyebrow or polite stare might serve to remind students to listen. If successful, the teacher has addressed the disruption without interrupting her or his directions. If this lowest level does not work, the teacher may move toward the students, stare more intently, or pause briefly to wait for silence. If these signals succeed, there has been little class interruption. If the students continue to talk, the teacher may address them directly "Bill and Joe, please listen to the discussion. Thank you." This hierarchy of messages continues until the problem is solved with as little disruption and as much dignity as possible. This process will be explained in detail in the next chapter.

Starting off by playing a very high card (making threats, sending to office, keeping after school, writing notes home) is often more trouble than the situation requires. The use of power in any relationship is seldom productive in terms of what it accomplishes over time. While power can produce immediate results, its continued use creates numerous negative side effects. Over-use of a strength becomes a weakness.

In order for a "low card" approach to work successfully, the teacher needs to have a sequence of "higher cards" to play as the situation demands. One such sequence involving students "talking while a teacher is giving directions" might be:

- raising eyebrows in an inquisitive fashion
- staring politely (steady gaze)
- pausing briefly while continuing to stare
- moving closer to the students while continuing to talk
- gently placing a hand on a student's desk while continuing to give directions to the class
- using the student's name as part of the lesson "Mary, What would be a good due date for our reports?"
- asking the student by name to listen to directions
- asking the student "What did I ask you to do?"
- asking the student to meet after class
- asking the student to move to a "time out" area in the room
- assigning penalties

As this sequence suggests, the point is to obtain the most results while expending the least amount of energy.

Honoring the net. As explained by Purkey and Schmidt (1987) the "net" is the hypothetical boundary between the teacher and student that marks an inviolable territory for each. This net concept is in keeping with the basic element or

DISCOURAGE EXCUSES. Excuses do not free us from responsibilities. We pay for everything in life, usually in advance. If students throw paper on the floor, they are expected to pick it up. If they miss school, they are expected to make up their work. "No excuses" shows respect for students' responsibilities and self-directing powers.♪

respect so central to Invitational Teaching. Respect is manifested in classroom rules of politeness and common civility. No teacher is ever too busy to practice courtesy.

In honoring the net, the teacher acknowledges the fact that he or she consists of only half of the sending/receiving process. No matter how much the teacher wishes for the student to accept his or her invitations, and, no matter how beneficial the opportunity, the teacher stays on one's own side of the net. In the final analysis, students are responsible for choosing their behaviors. It also follows that students are responsible for the logical consequences of their actions.

Ensuring reception. Many times opportunities to establish good discipline are missed simply because messages were sent but never received. Invitations are like letters – some get lost in the mail. It is the teacher's responsibility to make sure his or her messages have arrived. This involves some sort of request that the student acknowledge the message. It is vital that the teacher ensures that the content of the message is *received and acknowledged.* For example, the teacher might ask a student: "Joanne, what did I ask you to do?" Joanne may reply "I'm sorry, I didn't hear you." At this point, the teacher may could repeat the directions. Or, Joanne may say "I know. I'll get back to work." In either case, communication is re-established. Breakdowns in classroom communication can be reduced or avoided entirely if the teacher insures that accurate reception has occurred. Unless the content of a message is received and acknowledged, it remains meaningless.

Follow-up stage.

In the final stage of the good discipline process, teachers move beyond the initial preparation and Initiating/Responding Stages to work through the four steps of the Follow-up Stage:

(1) interpreting responses
(2) negotiating positions
(3) evaluating the process
(4) developing trust.

Interpreting responses. When the teacher describes what is needed for good classroom behavior, and his or her requests have been sent and acknowledged, the invitations become the property of the students receiving them. Students who have received the summons to behave themselves have the options of accepting, not accepting, rejecting, ignoring, modifying, or simply "tabling" them until another time. *What is important at this point is the teacher's interpretation of student responses*. If the student accepts the teacher's invitation, is the entire summons accepted or just part of it? Is the student aware of the responsibility embedded in the acceptance? In using a classroom good-behavior contract, for example, does everyone understand the obligations and consequences stated in the contract?

If a student indicates that the teacher's request to behave is rejected, was it in fact a rejection, or was it non-acceptance?

The two responses are sharply different. Sometimes students are unwilling or unable *at the moment* to accept the most well-meaning invitation, but this unwillingness does not necessarily mean rejection. For example, a student might be reluctant to participate in an academic activity not because he or she is stubborn, unruly, or wants to cause trouble, but because he or she is fearful of exposing a lack of ability. Rather than trying to pressure the student to participate, the teacher might ask the student to meet with the teacher alone to share concerns and feelings.

It is important for teachers to determine whether or not students are, in fact, rejecting their invitations. An apparent rejection of an invitation is often just the opposite. For example, one beginning teacher asked a student to help her move some supplies after class. "Are you kidding me?" the student replied, I've got more important things to do." The teacher was resentful because she assumed that her request had been rudely rejected. Later, she was startled when the student showed up to help. Some students will accept or reject invitations in their own ways and on their own terms. It is important to understand that acceptances come in many forms. Just as the person who extends an invitation determines the "rules" under which it is extended, the person receiving the invitation determines how it will be accepted.

Negotiating. Teachers who desire to invite good discipline but who encounter difficulties work to negotiate a way around them. Too often, teachers damage or even destroy Invitational Teaching's stance of trust, intentionality, respect, and optimism by being unwilling or unable to negotiate differences with students. Sometimes these differences begin as minor problems that could have easily been handled with some reasonable give and take.

An example might be useful here. On the door of a computer lab was a sign: NO FOOD OR DRINK IN THE COMPUTER LAB. (Although rudely worded, the directive makes sense, for computers are easily damaged.) A middle school student entered the lab chewing gum. The teacher expelled the student from the lab because he considered that gum is "food." The incident quickly became blown out of proportion when parents, school board members, administrators, and the local newspaper became involved in a nasty fight. The entire affair could have been avoided if the teacher had quietly requested that the student place the gum in the trashcan. It is easy to move from persuasion to coercion, but very difficult to move from coercion to persuasion. Once a high card in played, low cards mean little.

PROVIDE GUIDING QUESTIONS. When teachers give guiding suggestions, students have a structure for thinking through decisions yet continue to feel that they are involved in making choices. Questions such as " Have you considered ...?" What else might you have done...?" or "Did you try...?" reflect respect for the student's own self-directing powers.♪

Teachers are expected to maintain direction and purpose in their classrooms, but little is gained by holding doggedly to a rigid plan that cannot or will not be accepted by students. It is far more productive and conducive to a healthy classroom environment to seek and find reasonable alternatives that will be accepted by students, even if these plans do not meet immediate objectives. Accepting and completing an alternate plan that meets the needs of all parties involved frequently leads to a goal that surpasses the original objective.

A major part of negotiation is the teacher's ability to handle rejection. Invitational Teachers allow for the rejection of their requests, no matter how well-meaning and high-minded these requests might be. The teacher's responsibility should not deteriorate into student exploitation. While there should be logical consequences for good or bad behavior, the students' rights to participate in decisions that influence their lives are absolute.

But even when the summons to good behavior is rejected outright, it does not mean that the teacher has been rejected, that the invitation was worthless, or that every future invitation will be declined. There are countless reasons why students reject even the most beneficial of opportunities. Perhaps the student felt incapable of accepting ("I can't"), or perhaps the invitation is seen negatively ("I won't"). In either case, the rejection may be the student's way of eliciting an alternative invitation or testing the teacher's sincerity or commitment. Whatever the situation, the ultimate key to good discipline is continuing the inviting process – to hold one's stance.

Evaluating outcomes. As baseball's Yogi Berra often commented, "It ain't over 'till it's over," the same is true with good classroom discipline. Evaluation of the discipline process is essential. This may be done informally or

EVALUATE THE LESSON WITH A TWO-MINUTE SEMINAR. After a lesson has been presented, divide the class into pairs (randomly assign pairs to avoid cliques). Each pair is to talk over what has been presented for two minutes and write the key points on an index card. This lets the teacher know what students have learned, actively involves students, and keeps the lesson moving. ♪

formally. Informally, the teachers and students can hold a class discussion and analyze their progress in creating and maintaining a productive classroom environment. During this process it is important that the teacher be optimistic and not be unduly influenced by the concerns or complaints of a few students who may give an unbalanced perspective of classroom activities. A class meeting can clear the air and help enrich the classroom atmosphere.

Beyond the informal process of evaluation, the teacher can use various formal techniques such as recording over time the attendance and tardiness rates, the number of misbehavior episodes, homework return rate, standardized test scores, grade point averages, and other "objective" measures that may help gauge a productive classroom environment. But whether formal or informal, it is important that the teacher consistently evaluate the outcome of his or her classroom management techniques.

Developing trust. In creating and maintaining good discipline, any exchange in the classroom is but a single step in a long journey. Successful classroom management requires countless interactions, each serving as one more step towards the development of mutual trust.

FOCUS ON BEHAVIOR, NOT INTENTIONS. Teachers promote self-discipline by keeping the topic of conversation on action. For example, the question "Why did you trip Charlie?" may lead to all sorts of time-wasting, creative comments. A better question is "What did you do?" After attempting evasion, most students will admit to the undesirable activity. Once the behavior is admitted, the stage is set for the development of more socially appropriate behaviors. Again, the student is summoned to make choices and take responsibility. ♪

Trust is based on a combination of what has happened in the past, what is happening at the moment, and what is expected to happen in the future. While the teacher cannot do much about the student's past experiences other than helping some students to reinterpret them (these experiences happened, they are not happening), she or he can work to create a trusting environment for the present and future by following the steps outlined in this chapter.

The three-stages/twelve steps of the good discipline process have been highlighted in this chapter for the sake of understanding, but it is important to remember that good classroom discipline consists of myriad separate activities all happening simultaneously. *This is why it is so important for the teacher to have a consistent philosophy that guides behavior.* Without this internalized "gyrocompass," specific techniques and strategies will lack integrity. In this sense, good classroom management is the result of an overarching invitation to students to see themselves as able, valuable, and responsible, and to behave accordingly.

Summary

Invitational Teachers invite positive classroom discipline by connecting what they have learned regarding best practices with what they know about themselves and their students. Studies of successful classroom management emphasize the importance of self-discipline and Academic Learning Time. Researchers have also documented techniques that encourage both good discipline and academic achievement. Putting these techniques in action requires a high level of artistry that often results from our three-stage process of preparation, interaction, and follow up.

Invitational Teachers develop a stance grounded in their perceptions of students as valuable, able, and responsible. They work to create exciting, supporting environments for learning, and they consider the developmental needs of their students in making decisions. When disruptions occur, they play their "low cards" first and make sure that their signals to good discipline are received and acknowledged. When necessary, they play higher cards of negotiation and alternative discipline measures. They follow through on their decisions in ways that are caring, appropriate, and respectful to students. The result is a trusting and optimistic classroom environment that encourages students to learn self-discipline, even in the most difficult situations. Our final chapter describes inviting ways to manage conflicts. ♫

6

AN INVITATIONAL APPROACH TO CONFLICT MANAGEMENT

> When Yen ho was about to take up new duties as tutor to heir of a duke, he went to his teacher for advice. "I have to deal with a man of depraved and murderous disposition... how is one to deal with a man of this sort?" "I am glad that you asked this question. *The first thing you must do is not to improve him, but to improve yourself.*"
>
> — Bennis and Nanus (1985), Taoist story of ancient China

By increasing Academic Learning Time and using the strategies described in the good discipline sequence, Invitational Teachers can create classroom climates that promote self-discipline. Even so, conflicts will arise. Good and Brophy (2000) reported survey studies with middle school students that documented a wide variety of conflicts, ranging from rumors and gossip to verbal harassment and arguments to property destruction and physical fights (p. 175). They suggest that while conflicts are normal, students do not often know how to resolve them. Invitational Teachers can play an important role in helping students learn to address conflicts in productive ways rather than withdraw or resort to violence. Students can learn to employ strategies that permit them to pursue their own interests while preserving good relationships with their would-be "adversaries."

Knowing how to manage conflicts is important for teachers as well, not only with interactions with students, but also with colleagues and parents. When preventive discipline strategies do not work, or when students choose to be disruptive or hostile, teachers find themselves in conflict situations. By learning to manage conflicts productively, Invitational Teachers can continue to develop supportive relationships with students and show them that even the most difficult situations can be handled invitationally. This is the essence of leadership, and requires a different level of artistry. As teachers grow more adept at these leadership strategies, they find that their personal and professional lives are enriched accordingly.

LISTEN TO THE ICE. The fox in Esop's Fable avoided falling through the ice on the pond by listening to its sound. Successful teachers sense the mood of the class and avoid discipline problems before they happen by such means as moving towards the source of misbehavior, lowering one's voice, or shifting to a more interesting part of the lesson. They win the battle before it begins.♪

It may be useful to point out that Invitational Teaching requires a particular kind of assertiveness. This assertiveness is a clear affirmation that both teachers and students are to be treated with respect. The challenge is for the teacher to protect his or her rights as a person and teacher with the rights of students and others. As explained by Alberti and Emmons (1990), we only hurt ourselves, and ultimately other people, when we have a fatal desire to please: to behave in such a way as to never confront anyone under any circumstances. When teachers sacrifice their rights, they summon others to take advantage of them.

Beyond affirming one's own rights, Invitational Teaching also involves the ability to express feelings of appreciation and positive regard. It enables teachers to stand up for themselves without undue anxiety, to express feelings comfortably, and to exercise one's own rights without denying the rights of others. Invitational Teaching affirms one's own rights, in contrast to aggressive behavior, which is directed against others.

While assertiveness is healthy, the principles of Invitational Teaching (optimism, trust, respect, intentionality) help to safeguard the teacher from having assertiveness become hostility and aggression. Being human, teachers are sometimes tempted to run roughshod over people, particularly when they have the desire and power to do so. We have all known teachers who achieved a certain kind of classroom discipline through intentionally disinviting, orange-alert practices. However, in the final analysis, these individuals usually pay a high price for relying on raw power, denying the rights of others, and ignoring feelings.

Purkey and Novak (1996) have developed a systematic approach to conflict management that addresses and often solves problems in ways that maintain an invitational ethos of respect, trust, optimism, and intentionality. This chapter presents the six key levels of conflict management, known as the "Rule of the Six C's," and relates these levels to positive classroom discipline.

The Rule of the Six C's emphasizes that teachers and administrators benefit by managing conflicts at the lowest possible level, with the least amount of energy, and in a most respectful and appropriate manner. Whenever possible, they apply the lowest of the C Levels first and then move upward

KEEP PROBLEMS SIMPLE. When a student is misbehaving, try to avoid creating second level problems such as an angry exchange, a drawn-out explanation, or a counter complaint. Focus on the immediate behavior in a calm and deliberate manner, and seek to avoid an escalation of conflict. ♪

to more intensive strategies only as necessary. In this sense, the six levels are extensions of the "low card" concept introduced in the preceding chapter, structured more specifically to address the sensitive nature of conflict. The Six C's are concern, confer, consult, confront, combat, and conciliate.

Concern – Is this really a problem?"

As we mentioned earlier, in times of stress it is important to remain calm and proceed gently (Reed & Strahan, 1995). A "strong yet gentle" stance to conflict management begins with self-awareness. Before a teacher responds to a situation, he or she needs to decide whether or not what appears to be a conflict is really a concern. For example, there are times in the classroom when it is necessary to be quiet. At other times, it may not be a concern if students are talking and moving around. Here are some questions to consider when deciding whether or not a situation is a matter of concern:

1. Will this situation resolve itself without intervention?
2. Can this situation be safely and wisely overlooked without undue personal stress?
3. Does this situation involve a matter of ethics, legality, morality, or safety?
4. Is this the proper time to be concerned about this situation?

5. Is the situation a matter of concern because of my personal prejudices or biases?

Often, what might at first seem to be a concern proves to be simply a matter of preference. By pausing to ask these questions, a teacher may find that the concern will manage itself without intervention.

For example, two students may enter the room in what appears to be a heated argument. Taking a moment to reflect, the teacher remembers that these two students are friends and that they have had disagreements before. Rather than address the situation right away, the teacher walks closer and looks at them calmly. The students, still glaring at each other, take their seats and begin their warm-up activity. Five minutes later, they seem to have forgotten the disagreement.

CHECK YOUR TIMING. Few things are more important in good discipline than timing. Too much or too little, too soon or too late, can weaken the best intention. So ask yourself, "What invitation to good behavior is most likely to be accepted by this student at this moment?" Choosing the right moment for the right move is a hallmark of good teaching. ♪

The issue of concern is sometimes complex. One of the key questions asks us to consider ethical and legal issues. In this regard, "little things," like wearing a hat or chewing gum, may not be little things. Some teachers do not mind when students chew gum (and may even enjoy chewing gum themselves). They may not be inclined to notice chewing gum. However, if the school has a rule against gum, and the teacher decides to ignore the rule, he or she may send a message that "the rules do not apply in my class." While chewing gum may not

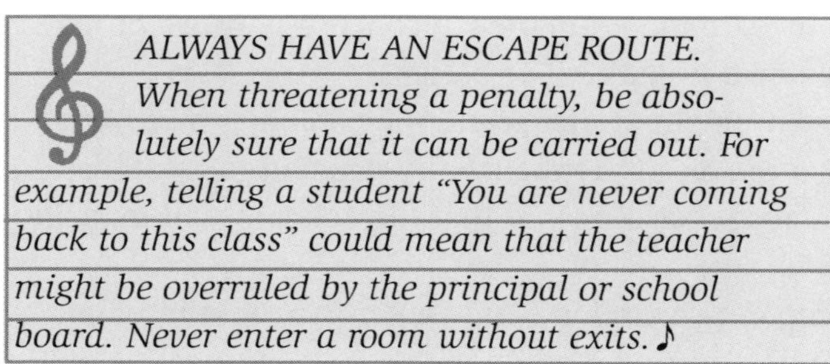
ALWAYS HAVE AN ESCAPE ROUTE. When threatening a penalty, be absolutely sure that it can be carried out. For example, telling a student "You are never coming back to this class" could mean that the teacher might be overruled by the principal or school board. Never enter a room without exits. ♪

interfere with learning, deciding that the gum is not a concern may put the teacher at odds with colleagues and send a "mixed message" to students. A "concerned" response would be to deal with gum chewing as a violation of the rules. The Invitational Teacher may then follow procedures to try to change the school-wide rule.

Taking time to consider "concern" is a natural extension of the "reading situations" step in the Good Discipline Sequence. It is also an opportunity to "expect good things" from others and ourselves.

Confer – Can we talk about this in private?

To confer means to initiate an informal conversation with the other person *in private.* This is the first step in the communication process. Having taken a moment to decide that the situation is, in fact, a matter of concern, and having tried to calm his or her emotional response, the teacher should ask the student (or whomever) to meet briefly in private to express the concern.

Conferring begins with the teacher reminding himself or herself to remain calm. As an ancient Chinese saying warns: "He who angers you controls you." Teachers calm students down with their own calmness, even when provoked by the behavior of others.

When expressing a concern, it is necessary for the teacher to focus on one issue at a time. Otherwise, the teacher will have to address several issues at once. *Counter-concerns can be considered after the original concern has been addressed.* This is not to imply that students are to be denied the right to express their concerns. In fact, not allowing students to express their concerns may increase their feelings of frustration and anger. However, *it is vital to address one concern at a time.* The teacher can ask students politely to "wait their turn" until the first concern is addressed. Choose the primary concern and stick to it until it is considered and, hopefully, resolved. This prevents skipping back and forth among issues, which could easily lead to an evasion of the original concern altogether.

In expressing the concern, the teacher should try to signal the desire for a positive and non-threatening dialogue. This can be done nonverbally with a smile, a relaxed posture, eye contact, or using the person's preferred name. As soon as possible, the teacher should state, in a caring and respectful manner, what the concern is, why it is a concern, and what is proposed to resolve the concern. For example, "Harry, you are late for class. Arriving late disrupts the learning process. Will you please arrive on time?" This straightforward message may resolve the matter. If not, it sets the stage for progressing to a higher level in as productive way as possible.

Questions to consider at the conferring level include:

1. After expressing concern, have I listened to encourage honest communication?
2. Is there a clear understanding by all parties regarding the nature of the concern?

3. Is there room for compromise or reconceptualization? (Perhaps the student is tardy because a previous class runs late. This may require other action).
4. Have I clearly asked for what I want? ("Will you do this for me?")
5. Most importantly, have I received voluntary verbal compliance?

As an illustration of this process, consider the teacher's options if the two students in an earlier scenario had not stopped arguing as class began. If they had continued to disagree or if they had begun to shout at each other, the teacher could ask to see them, one at a time, outside the room. Rather than ask, "What is the matter?" the teacher might begin by stating "When you enter the room loudly, it makes it difficult to get class started. Will you please enter the room quietly?" This approach allows the teacher to address the immediate disruption without entering a long discussion regarding why they were arguing.

> *OFFER THREE BLUE CARDS AND A WISH. A very "low card" to play in working to improve a student's behavior is to call that student aside and give three positive comments regarding his or her work, then quickly follow it up with your "wish". For example, "Marie, I am pleased with your work, and I like your enthusiasm and leadership. I do wish that you would get to class on time. Will you do this?" This is a very mild-mannered way of encouraging desirable student behavior.* ♪

By taking a few moments to be sure that he or she is calm and supportive, the teacher is a logical extension of the "preparing the setting" step of the good discipline sequence. Investing energy in "conferring" is an essential dimension of the Invitational Teaching stance. It also sends important messages to students that they are valuable, able to solve their problems, and responsible for their decisions. In most situations, a private, non-threatening, dialogue will resolve the situation or at least manage it for the time being. In other cases where conferring is insufficient, the situation merits consultation.

Consult – Do we remember our responsibilities?

Consultation is a more serious level of conversation with the focus shifting from an initial request to a discussion of a previous commitment. When the teacher has taken the time to confer, the student has probably agreed to a previous request to "grant the wish." If the situation persists (or returns), it becomes necessary to remind the student that he or she has made an agreement. At this point, the teacher should review with the student what was agreed upon and indicate, firmly and directly, that it is important to abide by that commitment. For example, in the situation in which Marie continues to arrive late to class, the teacher could say "Marie, you told me that you would be on time for class. Your word is very important to me. Now will you please get to class on time?" Questions that might guide consultation include:

1. Is it clear what is expected?
2. Is there room for compromise or reconceptualization?
3. Are there ways that I can assist the student to abide by previous commitments?

4. Is the concern important enough to move to a higher C if necessary?
5. Have the consequences of not resolving the conflict been considered?
6. Is there time to allow both parties to reflect on the concern before further action is taken?

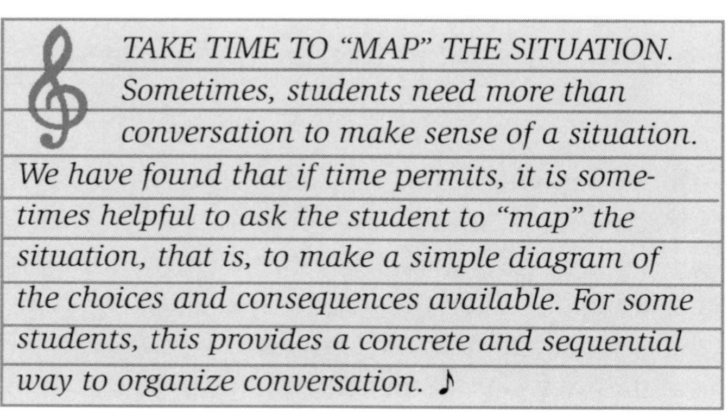

TAKE TIME TO "MAP" THE SITUATION. Sometimes, students need more than conversation to make sense of a situation. We have found that if time permits, it is sometimes helpful to ask the student to "map" the situation, that is, to make a simple diagram of the choices and consequences available. For some students, this provides a concrete and sequential way to organize conversation. ♪

Once again, Invitational Teaching affirms the conviction that people are valuable, able, and responsible. In cases where conferring did not work, and the intensity of confrontation is rising, the teacher has all the more reason to try to resolve the issue at this point. However, rising tensions should not change the teacher's stance. Even if the teacher is forced to proceed to confrontation, he or she can continue to approach the other person with respect, intentionality, optimism, and trust.

Confront – How can we connect choices and consequences?

At this level, the situation requires clear statements of logical consequences. The teacher can point out, in detail, what the concern is, why it is a concern, and what can be done about it. In doing so, the teacher can remind the student (or other person) that this situation has been addressed previously. The person gave his or her word that it would be resolved and has not kept that commitment.

For example, if Marie continues to arrive late to class, the teacher could say "Marie, you told me several times that you would be on time for class. Should you be late for class again, I will have to call your home and see what we can do about your tardiness." As another example, if the two students who tend to argue could not live up to their agreements, the teacher could meet with them individually and notify them that they might be separated (by seating or by scheduling) or that they may be required to participate in peer mediation or conflict management as a condition to continue in the class.

In the continuing effort to manage conflict as the lowest possible level, questions to consider at this confronting stage include:

1. Have sincere efforts been made to resolve the conflict at each of the previous three levels?
2. Is there documented evidence to show that earlier efforts have been made to resolve the conflict at each level?
3. Is there sufficient authority, power, and will to follow through on the consequences before they are stated?
4. Have all options been explored to obtain voluntary compliance?

At this point in the conflict management process it is helpful to reflect once again on the ethical stance of Invitational Teaching. Even in difficult situations, the teacher can demonstrate a caring commitment to the

HOLD YOUR POINT! Champion bird dogs are judged in part by how long they "hold the point" when they detect a covey of birds. Similarly, Invitational Teachers are judged by the way they consistently and dependably invite good discipline. Creating positive classroom discipline is a marathon, not a sprint. ♪

principles of Invitational Teaching. Moving to the combat stage requires an even deeper test of this commitment.

Combat – How can we enforce the consequences?

It may seem strange that this book advocates an invitational approach to classroom management, with its principles of respect, trust, optimism, and intentionality, and then presents the option of combat. To explain, we use the word "combat" as a verb rather than a noun. The goal is to combat the troublesome situation rather than to engage in combat with a person. The term combat is a reminder that the situation has reached a point that demands a resolution.

Because the conflict has not been resolved at each of the lower levels, it is now time to follow through on logical consequences. Up to his point, the Invitational Teacher has attempted to achieve a "win-win" solution. At the combat stage it can become a "win-lose" situation with much at stake in the outcome. When that happens, how the teacher wins is often as important as winning.

In preparing for combat situations, these questions are essential:

1. Is there clear documentation that other avenues were sought?
2. Have all lower levels of conflict management been honestly tried?
3. Even at this late date, is there a way to find room for compromise?
4. Are there sufficient support and resources available to successfully follow through on the consequences of combat?

5. Has the teacher sought help from fellow professionals (counselors, administrators, and school psychologists) before reaching this high level?

Or course, difficult situations sometimes require an almost immediate progression from concern to confer to consult to confront. If students engage in a "fist fight" or bring weapons to school, the teacher must act quickly to ensure safety. Even so, taking time to remind oneself to remain calm, to speak softly, to ask for cooperation, may prevent escalation.

Logical consequences are a fact of life. It would be unreasonable to think an Invitational Teacher can get along with persuasions and explanations alone. There are times when penalties are necessary, from the small reprimands to detentions and suspensions. But such actions should be based on real need and clear logic. Real need is established by the fact that all lower C's have been tried and have been unsuccessful in resolving the concern. Clear logic seeks to have the penalty make sense to the one being penalized. Efforts should be made to avoid having the person feeling wronged and resentful. The only avenue now open is to combat the situation. But even at this difficult stage the Invitational Teacher works to maintain respect for students.

A primary objective of a penalty is to have the offender reflect on the concern, realize what he or she did that was incorrect, and resolve not to do the same thing again. For example, a state trooper pulls us over for exceeding the posted speed limit. The state trooper introduces himself or herself, asks for identification, explains the offense and issues a citation. The cost of the speeding ticket is designed to discourage us from future speeding.

Notice here how a well-trained state trooper handles the situation. He or she demonstrates respect for the driver ("May I see your driver's license and auto registration, please?) and uses "sir" and "madam." When the person who received the ticket drives away, he or she may be angry, but the anger is usually directed toward oneself, not the state trooper. There is a vast difference between a state trooper and a storm trooper.

BE A SCUBA DIVER. Some authorities encourage teachers to take "a deep breath" to reduce tension. A better way is suggested by scuba divers who are taught to exhale all bad air before inhaling. The next time a student is getting on your nerves, slowly exhale the stale air from your lungs, and follow this with a gradual deep breath. It will reduce tension immediately. ♪

At the combat stage, it may be necessary to restrain students by calling immediately for assistance. *The time to learn how to take those actions is before they occur.* If a teacher is not sure what back-up systems are in place or what types of physical restraints are appropriate, he or she should request information from an administrator as soon a possible.

Conciliate – How can we reestablish a working relationship?

After the conflict has been managed, it is important that some healing takes place. Confrontations, and even combat, can be learning experiences. To re-establish working relationships and restore a non-combative atmosphere, the teacher should seek to keep in mind the long-term consequences of the confrontation. This reflection is a natural extension of the "follow-up stage" of the Good Discipline Sequence. The same principles apply: interpret responses, negotiate, evaluate outcomes, and develop trust. Questions to guide this follow-up include:

1. Is there the avoidance of "rubbing it in?"
2. Is there an attempt to allow the parties involved to have some time and space to adequately resume normal interactions?
3. Can helpful intermediaries be used?
4. Can non-threatening activities be used to restore a sense of inclusion?

In Chapter One we reported a scenario in which a teacher confronted a student for bringing a knife to school. We described how the teacher continued to support the student and his family during this situation and noted that the teacher spent a little extra time with the student when he came back from his suspension. This "extra time" was conciliation. Even though the student was angry about being suspended, he understood that the teacher was supporting him. By talking with the student privately, offering positive nonverbal signals, and including the student in lesson activities, the teacher was able to re-establish a caring relation-

DEMONSTRATE YOUR FALLIBILITY. A good way to develop trust in the class room is to have the courage to express one's own lack of knowledge in an area, or be able to apologize for some thoughtless act. By modeling that everyone is learning and that "no one is infallible" students are invited to risk making mistakes in order to develop optimally. ♪

ship with the student. Invitational Teachers act in a similar manner with students who have been involved in fights, or who have lost their tempers and "cussed out the teacher" in a heated moment, or who have engaged in other actions that have resulted in conflict. Conciliation is the "resolution" phase of conflict resolution. It re-affirms that everyone in the school is able, valuable, and responsible.

Teaching the Rule of the Six C's to students

The Rule of the Six C's provides a systematic framework for managing and resolving conflicts. This approach is practical as teachers and administrators can manage conflicts at the lowest possible level while expending the least amount of energy. It is invitational in its emphasis on trust, intentionality, respect, and optimism. Teaching this process to students gives them a practical, invitational strategy they can use to address concerns and conflict in their own lives, not only in school, but beyond.

We suggest teaching the Six C's as part of the curriculum. The six steps (concern, confer, consult, confront, combat, and conciliate) lend themselves to almost any method of problem solving that teachers employ in language arts, health, math, science, the arts, social studies, or science.

For example, the Six-C approach to conflict management is similar to the S.E.A.R.C.H. strategy for teaching problem solving developed by L'Esperance, Strahan, Farrington, and Anderson (in press):

> *Search the problem.*
>
> Students will write a single sentence that clearly describes the problem to be solved.

Evaluate what you already know.

Students will list aspects of the problem that they understand and identify questions they need to answer.

Arrange the facts.

Students will construct a diagram that explains the problem.

Reach a possible solution.

Students will present a first draft of their solution.

Check to see if it works.

Students will show how they tested and revised their solution.

Highlight main points to remember.

Students will prepare a summary to share with classmates. This could be a poster, paper or model. Students will then explain their work to a teacher.

This strategy can be incorporated into almost any aspect of the curriculum. The Rule of the Six C's and SEARCH provide ways to resolve or at least manage conflicts successfully.

To illustrate, a social studies teacher might ask students to use the Rule of the Six C's as a framework to analyze events leading up to the Civil War. Students could explore ways that some of the leaders on both sides attempted to avoid combat before and then tried to "conciliate" tensions after the war. In language arts, students might examine the conflicts that arise in a novel. In *The Outsiders* (Hinton, 1967), for example, the "Greasers" and the "Socs" engage in a number of conflicts. Students could analyze the ways that characters try to address these conflicts, noting when they employ some of the Rules of the Six C's and when they do not. Current issues in health and science lend themselves to this type of analysis as well. By incorporating the Rule of the Six C's into the curriculum, teachers can give students useful strategies for addressing conflicts in their lives as well as addressing conflicts in school more productively.

Conflict management and school culture: Leadership in action

In earlier chapters, we have described how the entire climate of the school contributes to student learning and to teachers' professional growth. In the "Jell-O Principle," we suggested that "the classroom and everybody in it is like one big bowl of Jell-O: if you touch it, the whole thing jiggles; everything is connected to everything else." The ways that conflicts are addressed (or not addressed) is an essential ingredient in school climate.

Fullan (1999) noted that in the most successful schools, students, teachers, parents, and administrators express disagreements in an open and productive manner:

> First, contrary to myth, effective collaborative cultures are not based on like-minded consensus. They value diversity because that is how they get different perspectives and access to ideas to address complex problems. Under such conditions, inequity is far less likely to go unnoticed or to be tolerated. At the same time, conflict is brought out into the open (p. 37).

Invitational Teachers help create more collaborative cultures by employing the Rule of the Six C's in their interactions with other adults in the building as well as with their students. Differences of opinion among colleagues can result in more creative solutions to problems. Conversations with parents can result in better understanding of students' needs as well as stronger collaboration. Disagreements regarding policies and procedures can lead to improvements. By employing the Rule of the Six C's, Invitational Teachers can encourage colleagues to identify matters of concern and to confer in a cooperative fashion. When tensions arise, they can consult with colleagues privately, confronting issues when necessary. When combat occurs, they can work to minimize the impact of "win-lose" scenarios and promote conciliation. The results are a more collaborative school culture.

Summary

In this chapter, we have presented a systematic approach to managing conflict. By following the Rule of the Six C's, Invitational Teachers create a classroom climate that promotes trust, intentionality, respect, and optimism. They encourage a school culture that features collaboration. At heart, the key questions that guide the Rule of the Six C's are

Concern – Is this really a problem?"
Confer – Can we talk about this in private?
Consult – Do we remember our responsibilities?
Confront – How can we connect choices and consequences?
Combat – How can we enforce the consequences?
Conciliate – How can we re-establish a working relationship?

These guiding principles re-affirm our commitment to make the school the "most inviting place in town," a place where students can learn to disagree productively, where adults can address matters of concern, where diversity is a source of strength, and where everyone cares for others and is cared for in return. In these inviting schools, positive discipline becomes a way of life and academic achievement thrives.

Conclusion

This small volume has presented theoretical concepts and practical ideas that should benefit students, teachers, and administrators in many different settings. Good classroom discipline is no accident; it is the result of respect, trust, and optimism, *intentionally* designed to ensure that each student is invited in some way each day. By offering "blue cards" and avoiding "orange practices" whenever possible, Invitational Teachers inform students that they valuable, able, and responsible and that they are expected to behave accordingly. Schools that connect people, places, policies, programs, and processes into a sense of community create cultures that promote self-discipline. Members of these caring communities invite themselves and others to become even more successful. The Good Discipline Sequence becomes a natural part of the school day, and students join teachers in learning to manage conflicts. Invitational Teachers blend together all of these ingredients in ways that meet the needs of their students and enhance their schools. Discipline becomes more than a chore; it becomes a positive part of the learning process. ♫

References

Amos, L. (1985). *Professionally and personally inviting teacher practices as related to affective course outcomes.* Doctoral dissertation. University of North Carolina at Greensboro.

Alberti, R. E., & Emmons, M. L. (1990). *Your perfect right: A guide to assertive behavior.* San Louis Obispo, CA: Impact Publishers.

Bateson, G. (1987). *Steps to an ecology of mind.* Northvale, NJ: Jason Aronson Press.

Beck, A. T. (1988). *Love is never enough.* New York: Harper & Row.

Bennis, W., & Nanus, B. (1985). *Leaders: The strategies for taking charge.* New York: Harper and Row.

Brophy, J. E. (1983). Classrooms organization and management, *The Elementary School Journal, 83* (4), 265-285.

Charles, C. (1992). *Building classroom discipline.* White Plains, NY: Longman.

Cirlot, J.E. (1962). *A dictionary of symbols.* New York: Philosophical Library.

Clark, S., Dunlap, G., Foster-Johnson, L., Childs, K., Wilson, D., White, R., & Vera, A. (1995). Improving the conduct of students with behavioral disorders by incorporating student interests into curricular activities. *Behavioral Disorders, 20* (4), 221-237.

Curwin, R. L., & Mendler, A. N. (1988). *Discipline with dignity.* Alexandria VA: Association for Supervision and Curriculum Development.

Duke, D. L., & and Jones, V. F. (1985). What can schools do to foster student responsibility? *Theory into Practice, 24* (4).

Fisher, C. W., Philby, N.N., Marliave, R., Cahen, L. S., Dishaw, M. M., Moore, J. E., & Berliner, D. C. (1978). *Teaching and learning in the elementary school: A summary of the beginning teacher evaluation study. Study Report VII-1.* San Francisco, CA: Far West Laboratory for Educational Research and Development.

Frankl, V. (1968). *From psychotherapy to logotherapy.* New York: Knopf. (Reprinted 1986 by Random House).

Fullan, M. (1999). *Change forces: The sequel.* London: Falmer Press.

Gladding, S. T. (1992). *Counseling A comprehensive profession* (2nd ed.). New York: Merrill.

Glasser, W. (1965). *Reality therapy: A new approach to psychiatry.* New York: Harper and Row.

Glasser, W. (1974). A new look at discipline. *Learning, 3* (4), 6-11.

Glasser, W. (1986). *Control theory in the classroom.* New York: Harper and Row.

Glasser, W. (1993). *The quality school teacher*. New York: Harper Perennial.

Good, T., & Brophy, J. (1980). *Educational psychology: A realistic approach.* New York: Holt, Rinehart & Winston.

Good, T., & Brophy, J. (1984). *Looking in classrooms.* New York: Harper & Row.

Good, T., & Brophy, J. (2000). *Looking in classrooms* (8th ed.). New York: Longman.

Gouldner, H. (1978). *Teachers' pets, troublemakers, and nobodies*. Westport, CT: Greenwood Press.

Hattie, J. (1992). *Towards a model of schooling: A synthesis of meta-analyses.* Australian Journal of Education, 36, 5-13.

Hattie, J. (1996, April). *Future directions in self-concept research.* Paper presented at the annual meeting of the American Educational Research Association. New York.

Hattie, J., Jaeger, R., Strahan, D., & Baker, W. (1998). *Report on the development of the assessment/data collection instruments and protocols.* Unpublished manuscript, Center for Educational Research and Evaluation, University of North Carolina at Greensboro.

Hayakawa, S. I. (1990). *Language in thought and action* (5th ed.). Washington, DC: Harcourt, Brace & Jovanovich.

Hinton, S.E. (1967). *The outsiders.* New York: Dell Publishing Co., Inc.

Hockaday, S., Purkey, W. W., and Davis, K. (2001). Intentionality in helping relationships: The influence of three forms of internal cognitions on behavior. *The Journal of Humanistic Counseling, Education, and Development, 40* (2), 219-224.

Johnston, H. J. (with J. Maria Ramos de Perez). (1985, January). Four climates of effective middle schools. *Schools in the Middle.* National Association of Secondary School Principals.

Jones, V. (1996). Classroom management. In J. Sikula (Ed.), *Handbook of research on teacher education* (2nd ed.) (pp. 503-524). New York: Simon & Schuster Macmillan.

Keen, S. (1983). *The passionate life: Stages of loving.* San Francisco: Harper.

Kounin, J. (1970). *Discipline and group management in classrooms.* New York: Holt, Rinehart, and Winston.

L' Esperance, M., Strahan, D., & Farrington, V. (2001). Nurturing school culture and raising achievement through dialogue: A case study in middle school reform. International *Journal of Educational Reform, 10* (1), 46-63.

L' Esperance, M., Strahan, D., Farrington, V., & Anderson, P. (In press). *Project Genesis: Creating a middle school of significance in the 21st century.* Westerville, OH: National Middle School Association.

Manning, J. (1959). Discipline in the good old days. *Phi Delta Kappan, 42* (3), 87-91.

Maslow, A. (1970). *Motivation and personality* (2nd ed.). New York: Harper & Row.

McGinnis, A. L. (1979). *The friendship factor.* Minneapolis, MN: Augsburg Publishing House

Meichenbaum, D. (1977). *Cognitive-behavior modification: An integrated approach.* New York: Plenum.

Miller, D., & Hoy, W. (2000). A culture of openness: Toward a model of middle school effectiveness. *Research in Middle Level Education Annual, 23*, 49-64.

Novak, J. M. (1992). Critical imagination for invitational theory, research and practice. *Journal of Invitational Theory and Practice, 1* (2), 77-86.

Novak, J. M. (Ed.). (1992). *Advancing invitational thinking.* San Francisco: Caddo Gap Press.

Novak, J. M. (1994). Introduction: the talk and walk of democratic teacher education. In J. M. Novak (Ed.), *Democratic teacher education: Programs processes, problems, and prospects* (pp. 253-255). Albany, NY: State University of New York Press.

Novak, J. (2002). *Inviting educational leadership: Fulfilling potential and applying an ethical perspective to educational process.* London: Pearson Education Publishers.

Purkey, W. W. (1978) *Inviting school success: a self-concept approach to teaching and learning.* Belmont, CA: Wadsworth.

Purkey, W. W. (2000). *What students say to themselves: Internal dialogue and school success.* Thousand Oaks, CA: Corwin Press, Inc.

Purkey, W. W., & Gerber, S. (1997). Great wizard or good witch? *Journal of Humanistic Education and Development. 36,* 100-104.

Purkey, W. W., & Novak, J. M. (1984). *Inviting school success: A self-concept approach to teaching and learning* (2nd ed.). Belmont, CA: Wadsworth.

Purkey, W. W., & Novak, J. M. (1996). *Inviting school success: A self-concept approach to teaching and learning* (3rd ed.). Belmont, CA; Wadsworth.

Purkey, W. W., & Schmidt, J. (1987). *The inviting relationship: An expanded perspective for professional counseling.* Englewood Cliffs, NJ: Prentice-Hall, Inc.

Purkey, W. W., & Schmidt, J. (1996). *Invitational counseling: A self-concept approach to professional practice.* Pacific Grove, CA: Brooks/Cole Publishing Company.

Purkey, W. W., & Stanley, P. H. (1991). *Invitational teaching, learning, and living.* Washington, DC: National Education Association.

Purkey, W., W., & Strahan, D. (1986). *Positive discipline: A pocketful of ideas.* Columbus, OH: National Middle School Association.

Purkey, W., & Strahan, D. (1995). School transformation through Invitational Education. *Research in the Schools, 2* (2) 1-6.

Reed, C., & Strahan, D. (1995). Gentle discipline in violent times. *Journal for a Just and Caring Education, 1* (3), 320-334.

Roeser, R., Eccles, J., & Sameroff, A. (2000). School as a context of early adolescents' academic and socio-emotional development: A summary of research findings. T*he Elementary School Journal, 100* (5), 443-471.

Saint-Exupéry, A. de (1943). *The little prince.* New York: Harcourt, Brace & World.

Schmidt, J. (1994). *Living intentionally and making life happen* (rev. ed.) Greenville, NC: Brookcliff Publishers.

Simpson, A. W., & Erickson, M. T. (1983). Teachers' verbal and nonverbal communications patterns as a function of teacher race, student gender, and student race. *American Educational Research Journal, 20* (2), 193-198.

Smith, T. W. (1999). *Toward a prototype of expertise in teaching: A descriptive case study.* Doctoral dissertation, UNC Greensboro.

Stanley, P. H. (1992). A bibliography for invitational theory and practice. *Journal of Invitational Theory and Practice, 1* (1), 52-69.

Stanley, P., & Purkey, W. (1994). Student self-concept as learner: Does Invitational Education make a difference? *Research in the Schools, 1* (2) 15-22.

Strahan, D. (1994). Putting middle level perspectives into practice: Creating school cultures that promote caring. *Midpoints, 5* (1), 1-12.

Tinker v. Des Moines Independent Community School District, U.S. 503 & 511, 393 (1969).

Van Hoose, J., Strahan, D., & L'Esperance, M. (2001). *Promoting harmony: Young adolescent development and school practices.* Westerville, Ohio: National Middle School Association.

Wang, M., Haertel, G., & Walberg, H. (1993) Toward a knowledge base for school learning. *Review of Educational Research, 63* (3), 249-294.

Wolcott, H. K. (1999). *Ethnography: A way of seeing*. Walnut Creek, CA: Alta Mira Press.

National Middle School Association

National Middle School Association, established in 1973, is the voice for professionals and others interested in the education and well-being of young adolescents. The association has grown rapidly and enrolls members in all 50 states, the Canadian provinces, and 42 other nations. In addition, 56 state, regional, and provincial middle school associations are official affiliates of NMSA.

NMSA is the only association dedicated exclusively to the education, development, and growth of young adolescents. Membership is open to all. While middle level teachers and administrators make up the bulk of the membership, central office personnel, college and university faculty, state department officials, other professionals, parents, and lay citizens are members and active in supporting our single mission – improving the educational experiences of 10-15 year olds. This open and diverse membership is a particular strength of NMSA's.

The association publishes *Middle School Journal,* the movement's premier professional journal; *Research in Middle Level Education; Middle Ground, the Magazine of Middle Level Education; Target,* the association's newsletter; *The Family Connection,* a newsletter for families; *Classroom Connections,* a practical quarterly resource; and a series of research summaries.

A leading publisher of professional books and monographs in the field of middle level education, NMSA provides resources both for understanding and advancing various aspects of the middle school concept and for assisting classroom teachers in planning for instruction. More than 70 NMSA publications are available through the resource catalog as well as selected titles published by other organizations.

The association's highly acclaimed annual conference, which has drawn approximately 10,000 registrants in recent years, is held in the fall. NMSA also sponsors an annual urban education conference and a number of weekend workshops and institutes.

For information about NMSA and its many services, contact the association's headquarters office at 4151 Executive Parkway, Suite 300, Westerville, Ohio, 43081. TELEPHONE: 800-528-NMSA; FAX: 614-895-4750; INTERNET: www. nmsa.org.